Wisconsin Birds

A Seasonal and Geographical Guide

Wisconsin Birds

A Seasonal and Geographical Guide

Second Edition

Stanley A. Temple
John R. Cary
and
Robert E. Rolley

Sponsored by
The Wisconsin Society for Ornithology
and the Wisconsin Department of Natural Resources

The University of Wisconsin Press

A North Coast Book

The University of Wisconsin Press
2537 Daniels Street
Madison, Wisconsin 53718

3 Henrietta Street
London WC2E 8LU, England

Printed in the United States of America

Library of Congress Cataloging-in-Publication Data
Temple, Stanley A., 1946–
    Wisconsin Birds: a seasonal and geographical guide / Stanley A.
Temple, John R. Cary, and Robert E. Rolley. — 2nd ed.
    320 pp.   cm.
    ''Sponsored by the Wisconsin Society for Ornithology and the
Wisconsin Department of Natural Resources.''
    Includes bibliographical references and index.
    ISBN 0-299-15220-0 (cloth: alk. paper).
    ISBN 0-299-15224-3 (pbk.: alk. paper)
    1. Bird watching—Wisconsin. 2. Birds—Wisconsin—Geographical
distribution. 3. Birds—Wisconsin—Geographical distribution—Maps.
I. Cary, John R. (John Robert), 1946–   . II. Rolley, Robert E.
III. Wisconsin Society for Ornithology. IV. Wisconsin. Dept of
Natural Resources. V. Title.
QL684. W5T46   1997
598'.07'234775—dc21   97-37410

To the dedicated amateur ornithologists who have reported their weekly observations of Wisconsin birds on over 65,000 checklists submitted during the past fifteen years.

Contents

Acknowledgments

Publication of this book was made possible by the enthusiastic cooperation of Wisconsin birders, most of them members of the Wisconsin Society for Ornithology, who have reported their weekly bird observations since 1982. Funding for the Wisconsin Checklist Project has come from the A. W. Schorger Fund of the Department of Wildlife Ecology at the University of Wisconsin–Madison, the Beers-Bascom Professorship in Conservation, which is held by the senior author, the Wisconsin Department of Natural Resources (WDNR) Fish and Wildlife Conservation Segregated Fund, the WDNR Endangered Resources Fund, and Federal Aid in Wildlife Restoration Project W-141-R. For the first seven years of the project, Anita J. Temple took care of correspondence with the volunteers and kept track of the tens of thousands of checklists they submitted. Gerald A. Bartelt, Brian J. Dhuey, John J. Huff, and Madell T. Jackson II assisted with administration of the project after its transfer to the WDNR.

Preface to the Second Edition

The Wisconsin Checklist Project, now 16 years old, has repeatedly demonstrated its utility in describing the status of bird populations in Wisconsin. Begun in 1982 under the sponsorship of the Wisconsin Society for Ornithology, the checklist project has been administered by the Wisconsin Department of Natural Resources since 1989. The first edition of this book, which appeared in 1987, summarized the initial five years of the project. Now, a decade later, the project has accumulated much more data on Wisconsin birds, allowing for refinements in some of the patterns described in the first edition and new analyses not possible during the early phases of the project.

Perhaps of most significance is the addition of long-term trend data in the second edition. These analyses, based on 14 years of the project's data (1983–96), reveal how the status of birds has changed in Wisconsin. They corroborate and, in some cases, provide new insights into patterns revealed by other monitoring efforts, such as the North American Breeding Bird Survey and the Christmas Bird Count.

Our enthusiasm over the products of the checklist project and the processes that produced them remains high. This project is an outstanding example of how dedicated amateur ornithologists make an important contribution to our understanding of birds. Its value increases as more data are contributed. We hope readers will agree and that they will be motivated to contribute to this important project.

Preface to the First Edition

There are millions of dedicated birdwatchers in the United States, and these amateur ornithologists spend hundreds of millions of hours in the field observing birds each year. Professional ornithologists have long coveted such an army of field observers, and they have often tried to enlist the assistance of birders in collecting data that could be used to monitor changes in bird populations or to test scientific hypotheses. For a variety of reasons, the courtship of the amateur by the professional has not gone smoothly. Professionals have frequently asked too much of the amateur, and amateurs have, as a result, quickly lost interest in collecting data. Amateurs are often motivated to participate in programs that provide information of direct utility in birdwatching, but they are often less interested in research that is related to conservation or pure science.

The research project that produced the material in this book seems to have overcome many of the problems that have plagued other research ventures involving cooperation between amateur and professional ornithologists. The demands placed on the participating birdwatchers, have been few; the information they have provided can be used to study important aspects of the population biology of birds; and the results can be of direct interest to the birdwatchers themselves, as this book attests. We are, therefore, pleased to present here some of the results of the Wisconsin Checklist Project. We hope the birdwatchers of Wisconsin will be encouraged to see that their field activities can make a worthwhile contribution to ornithology and that professional and amateur ornithologists can work together to produce results of interest to both.

Introduction

What are the chances of finding a particular species of bird in Wisconsin? When and where is each species most likely to be encountered? How has the abundance of a species changed over time? These questions are of perennial interest to birdwatchers, and in this book we have attempted to answer them in a novel way: by systematically analyzing records that have been kept by Wisconsin birdwatchers themselves.

This book presents the results of the Wisconsin Checklist Project, which uses simple checklist information provided by volunteer observers to produce information on bird populations in Wisconsin. Participants in the project submitted weekly checklists of the birds they had encountered in their respective regions of the state. From these records we calculated reporting frequencies (the percentage of the weekly checklists on which the species had been reported during a particular period of time and in a particular region of Wisconsin). These reporting frequencies became the basis for seasonal, geographical, and historical analyses of the distributions and abundances of bird populations in Wisconsin. A more detailed description of the Wisconsin Checklist Project is provided in the Appendix.

The book consists of single-page species accounts for the 266 bird species most commonly found in Wisconsin. Each account presents in graphic format information on the probability of seeing the species in Wisconsin, the geographical range and abundance of the species within the state, seasonal changes in abundance that occur during the year, based on 1982–96 data, and the trend in abundance over the past 14 years, based on 1983–96 data.

In addition to the 266 species covered here, there are 98 other species that are found so infrequently in the state that the checklist methodology would not adequately describe their status. Information on these birds can be found in Robbins (1991).

ARRANGEMENT OF THE SPECIES ACCOUNTS

Information contained in each of the 266 full-page species accounts is presented in a standard format. A sample page —in this case presenting information for the Purple Martin —is shown in Figure 1. The common and scientific names given for each species are those published by the American Ornithologists' Union (1983 and subsequent revisions). Each account includes a graph showing the probability of finding the species in Wisconsin during an average year, either one or two range maps, a seasonal abundance graph, and a graph of the trend in reporting frequencies. In the following sections of this Introduction we describe how to interpret these features of the species accounts.

PROBABILITY OF FINDING THE SPECIES IN WISCONSIN

This graph shows the average probability of finding a bird of a given species in Wisconsin during a typical year and provides a way of gauging how common or rare a particular bird is in the state. The higher the value on the bar graph (from 0% on the left to 100% on the right), the more common the bird is and the more likely you are to find it.

To produce this graph we calculated the average percentage of participants in the checklist project who reported the species at least once during each year of the program. The most common species—such as the American Crow (page 80)—were reported by almost every participant each year and, hence, scored nearly 100% on the bar graph. You are almost certain to see these common species in Wisconsin

Purple Martin
Progne subis

Annual probability (%) of sighting this species in Wisconsin

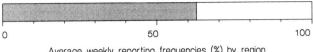

Average weekly reporting frequencies (%) by region

Average weekly reporting frequencies (%) during year

Changes in average weekly reporting frequencies (%) 1983-1996

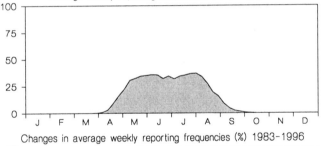

Figure 1. An example of a typical species account: the Purple Martin.

during a typical year. In contrast, the Red-throated Loon (page 31)—a rarer species—was reported by only 3% of the project participants each year. Your chances of seeing the bird in Wisconsin are, therefore, likely to be low. In the example in Figure 1, the shaded portion of the graph shows that, on average, 63% of the cooperating observers reported Purple Martins at least once each year. Thus, the Purple Martin was a moderately common species in Wisconsin; the average birdwatcher had a 63% chance of finding it during a typical year.

THE RANGE MAPS

For each species we have constructed either one or two range maps that show the distribution and geographical pattern of abundance of the bird in the state. For a bird that is a permanent year-round resident, there is a single map showing its range throughout the year. For a migratory bird present during only one season of the year, there is a single range map. For partial migrants that are always present somewhere in Wisconsin but whose distribution in the state changes with the seasons, there are two range maps, one for the breeding season and another for the nonbreeding season. For species that only pass through Wisconsin during spring and fall migrations, spring and fall distribution maps are provided. The actual time period covered by each map is indicated at the top of the map.

To produce the range maps, we divided the state into 56 regions, as delineated in Figure 2. Because participants in the checklist project were not evenly distributed among the 72 counties in Wisconsin, some counties, particularly in sparsely populated northern Wisconsin, were underrepresented. In such instances, we combined records from adjacent counties to create regions containing an adequate number of reports. The resulting 56 regions were composed of 42 individual counties plus 14 regions created by mergers. The counties of Wisconsin are shown in Figure 3.

Shaded portions of each range map show the counties or

18

regions where the bird has been reported during the check-list project. In addition to showing where the bird has been found in Wisconsin, the range maps show geographical patterns of abundance within each bird's range. The heaviest shading indicates regions in which the species is particularly common, the medium shading shows areas of moderate abundance, and the lightest shading shows areas where the bird is present but relatively scarce. These three levels of relative abundance were determined on the basis of the reporting frequencies in each of the geographical regions where a species had been reported. Regional reporting frequencies for each species were arranged in increasing order. The regions in the top quarter of the list have the heaviest shading, those in the bottom quarter of the list the lightest shading, and those in the middle half of the list the medium shading. The legend in the lower left corner of each map shows the average weekly reporting frequencies associated with each of the three levels of shading. In the case of the Purple Martin (Figure 1), the heaviest shading corresponds to reporting frequencies greater than 18.2%, the medium shading to 7.5-18.2%, and the lightest shading to less than 7.5%.

The range maps can be used to determine where a particular bird can be found in the state and where within its range it is relatively common or scarce. Keep in mind, however, that the levels of shading in these range maps should not be used to compare the relative abundance of different birds. A bird that is not often seen in Wisconsin may, nevertheless, be more common in one region of the state than another. Even in the regions where it is most common, however, it may still be quite uncommon in comparison to other more abundant species.

The geographical ranges and patterns of abundance for many bird species in Wisconsin are closely associated with the distribution of major ecosystems. Wisconsin can be divided broadly into two major ecological regions: the northern forest region and the southern forest-prairie

Figure 2. The 56 regions of Wisconsin used to analyze geographical distribution and abundance.

Figure 3. The counties of Wisconsin.

region (Curtis 1959). These two major regions are separated from each other by a zone of transition that is called the "tension zone" (Figure 4). Within the tension zone there occurs a dramatic change in the composition of plant and animal communities. You will notice on the various range maps that the geographical distributions of many birds show a marked change of abundance in the vicinity of the tension zone. These are birds that are closely tied to one or the other of the state's major ecological regions. The Boreal Chickadee (page 183) is most abundant north of the tension zone whereas the Tufted Titmouse (page 184) is most abundant to the south.

SEASONAL PATTERNS OF ABUNDANCE

The abundance of every species of bird in Wisconsin varies to some extent during the year. Populations of migrants change dramatically as individuals pass through the state on their seasonal movements, and populations of resident species change more subtly as a result of seasonal reproduction and mortality. In each species account we provide graphs that show how the average weekly reporting frequencies for the species varied throughout the typical year. A weekly reporting frequency of 100% would mean that every participant in the checklist project reported the species during that week. You should note that graphs for different species sometimes have different scales, so caution is in order when comparing the seasonal patterns between species.

The graphs of seasonal abundance can be used to determine when a species is found in the state, when the peaks of migration occur, and when migrants have finished their passage through the state and only residents remain. For example, Figure 1 indicates that the Purple Martin is a summer resident in Wisconsin; its abundance increases through April and early May when migrants move into the state. Its abundance is fairly stable through the summer but then

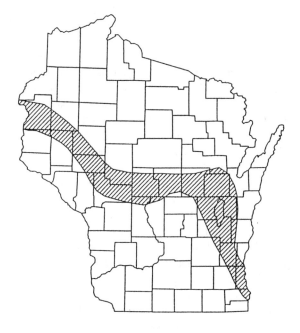

Figure 4. The "tension zone" within which there is a rapid transition between northern and southern plant and animal communities (after Curtis 1959).

declines through August and September as birds migrate south.

POPULATION TREND GRAPHS

Because the checklist project has accumulated information on Wisconsin birds over a period of many years, it is possible to detect trends in reporting frequencies over time. As a population increases or decreases in abundance, average reporting frequencies rise or fall. Year-to-year differences in average weekly reporting frequencies track population changes and provide a way to detect long-term trends. Over the 14-year period, 1983–96, analyzed in this book, some species have become more abundant while others have declined or fluctuated. The Purple Martin, for example, has been declining, according to the graph in Figure 1.

The average weekly reporting frequency for each year is shown as a point on the graph, while the line shows the overall trend, as determined by a regression analysis. In the case of the Purple Martin, the average weekly reporting frequency was highest in 1983 (16%) and lowest in 1995 (10%). The overall trend suggests that reporting frequencies for martins have declined by about 5% over the period covered by the checklist project. Other species, such as the Canada Goose (page 48), have increased, and some birds, such as the Northern Goshawk (page 79), have undergone cyclic fluctuations. In the case of the goshawk, the population has undergone an expected 10-year cycle of abundance in Wisconsin, with high reporting frequencies in 1984 and 1993 and low reporting frequencies in 1988.

A CAUTIONARY NOTE

The results of the checklist project have made it possible for us to produce an informative series of species accounts for most of the birds in Wisconsin. These accounts are far more quantitative than anything previously available. There are, however, some aspects of these results that must be interpreted cautiously.

There is the basic assumption that the reporting frequency for a species is closely correlated with its abundance. Although there can be no doubt that this assumption is basically valid, reporting frequencies can also be influenced by factors other than a species' absolute abundance. Conspicuousness of the bird—how easy it is to detect—can influence the ability of observers to discover a bird and, hence, can affect reporting frequencies.

An example of this problem is the difference between reporting frequencies of some warblers—such as the Magnolia Warbler (page 225)—in spring and fall. In the spring, migrant warblers are in conspicuous breeding plumage, and many trees have not yet leafed out. In the fall, migrant warblers are in dull nonbreeding plumage, and their passage often occurs before trees have lost their leaves. Accordingly, warblers are easier to observe and reporting frequencies are higher in spring than in fall. Logically, however, we must acknowledge that there are more warblers in the fall than in the spring. The fall populations have been bolstered by the summer's reproduction, whereas spring populations have been depleted by overwinter mortality. Similarly, spring reporting frequencies are elevated for birds, such as the Ruffed Grouse, Wild Turkey, and Northern Bobwhite, that have conspicuous breeding displays.

Other examples are the Downy and Hairy Woodpeckers (pages 157 and 158). These woodpeckers are regular users of bird feeders during the winter, but they are dispersed in surrounding forests during the summer. As a result, they are seen and reported more frequently in winter than in summer, even though there are more woodpeckers in summer because of the addition of young birds to the population.

The changes in reporting frequencies shown in population trend graphs may be affected by factors other than actual changes in population levels. Increases in the expertise and mobility of birders and the quality of the equipment they use could lead to higher reporting frequencies for some species. Changes in the proportion of participants who actively search for birds could also affect reporting rates. Reporting frequencies could also increase when new birding areas inhabited by a species are added to birders' itineraries in the state.

The range maps we constructed for each species probably tend, to some extent, to portray the range of a species as slightly larger than it actually is. The boundaries of the range maps are set by the boundaries of the regions we used for analysis, but the actual boundaries of a species' range, of course, do not necessarily correspond to these geopolitical units. For example, some aquatic birds, such as the Red-throated Loon (page 31), that are found along the shore of Lakes Michigan and Superior appear to be distributed farther inland than is actually the case.

The geographical patterns of relative abundance for species that are relatively uncommon but widespread are perhaps not as reliable as those for species that are more common. For species for which we do not have many reports, the regions of the state where the species is depicted as relatively more abundant may actually have had only a few more reports than other areas. For example, there is little difference in the regional reporting frequencies of the relatively uncommon Red-throated Loon (page 31). Slight regional differences can also be further accentuated by the tendency of birdwatchers to flock to a site where an uncommon bird has been reported by other observers, and this behavior artificially inflates its reporting frequency.

Because birdwatchers differ in the intensity of their field activities, reporting frequencies will be higher in regions with many active birders than in regions with many passive birders whose checklists may reflect only birds seen in their backyards. We suspect that this variation in the behavior of birders explains why some adjacent regions have different reporting frequencies, even though the actual abundance of the bird is probably similar.

REFERENCES

American Ornithologists' Union. 1983. *Check-list of North American birds* (6th ed.). American Ornithologists' Union, Washington, D.C.

Curtis, J. T. 1959. *The vegetation of Wisconsin.* University of Wisconsin Press, Madison.

Robbins, S. D. 1991. *Wisconsin birdlife: population and distribution, past and present.* University of Wisconsin Press, Madison.

Species Accounts

Red-throated Loon
Gavia stellata

Annual probability (%) of sighting this species in Wisconsin

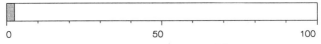

0   50   100

Average weekly reporting frequencies (%) by region

All Months

□ no report
□ < 0.1
▨ 0.1–0.4
■ > 0.4

Average weekly reporting frequencies (%) during year

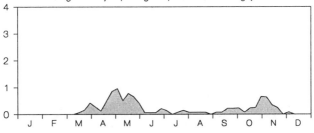

Changes in average weekly reporting frequencies (%) 1983–1996

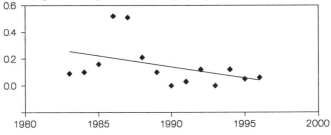

Common Loon
Gavia immer

Annual probability (%) of sighting this species in Wisconsin

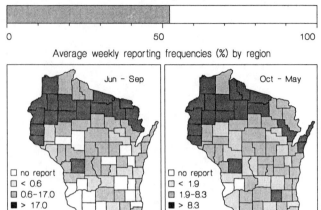

Average weekly reporting frequencies (%) by region

Jun – Sep

□ no report
□ < 0.6
▦ 0.6-17.0
■ > 17.0

Oct – May

□ no report
□ < 1.9
▦ 1.9-8.3
■ > 8.3

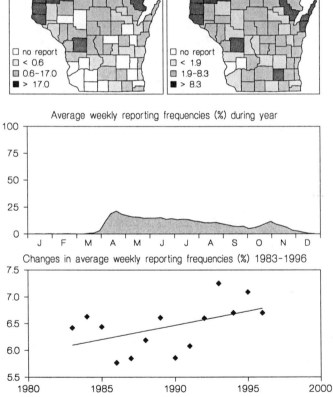

Average weekly reporting frequencies (%) during year

Changes in average weekly reporting frequencies (%) 1983-1996

Pied-billed Grebe
Podilymbus podiceps

Annual probability (%) of sighting this species in Wisconsin

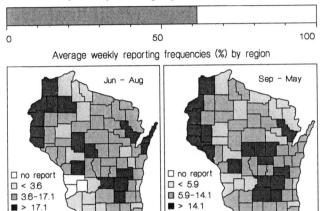

Average weekly reporting frequencies (%) by region

Jun – Aug

Sep – May

□ no report
□ < 3.6
▨ 3.6–17.1
■ > 17.1

□ no report
□ < 5.9
▨ 5.9–14.1
■ > 14.1

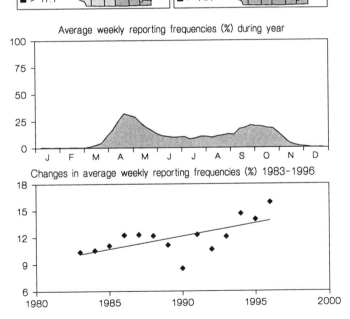

Average weekly reporting frequencies (%) during year

Changes in average weekly reporting frequencies (%) 1983–1996

Horned Grebe
Podiceps auritus

Annual probability (%) of sighting this species in Wisconsin

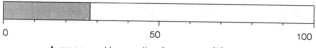

0   50   100

Average weekly reporting frequencies (%) by region

All Months

- □ no report
- ☐ < 0.5
- ▨ 0.5-2.4
- ■ > 2.4

Average weekly reporting frequencies (%) during year

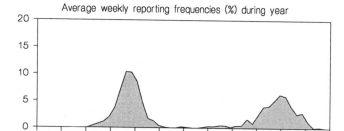

Changes in average weekly reporting frequencies (%) 1983-1996

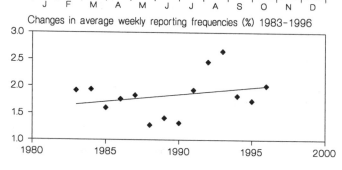

Red-necked Grebe
Podiceps grisegena

Annual probability (%) of sighting this species in Wisconsin

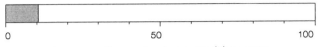

| 0 | 50 | 100 |

Average weekly reporting frequencies (%) by region

Average weekly reporting frequencies (%) during year

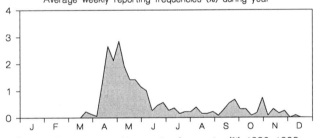

Changes in average weekly reporting frequencies (%) 1983-1996

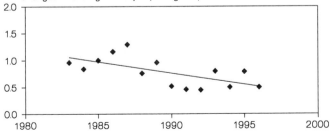

Double-crested Cormorant
Phalacrocorax auritus

Annual probability (%) of sighting this species in Wisconsin

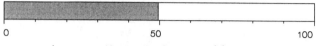

0   50   100

Average weekly reporting frequencies (%) by region

All Months

- □ no report
- □ < 1.5
- ▨ 1.5–11.7
- ■ > 11.7

Average weekly reporting frequencies (%) during year

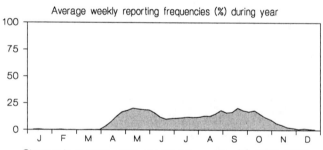

Changes in average weekly reporting frequencies (%) 1983-1996

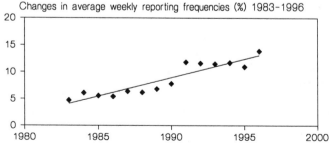

American Bittern
Botaurus lentiginosus

Annual probability (%) of sighting this species in Wisconsin

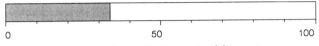

| 0 | 50 | 100 |

Average weekly reporting frequencies (%) by region

All Months

□ no report
□ < 0.8
▨ 0.8-5.6
■ > 5.6

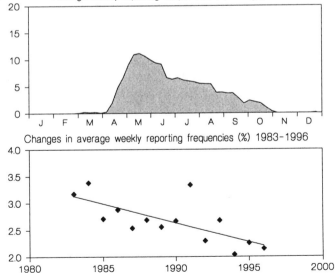

Average weekly reporting frequencies (%) during year

Changes in average weekly reporting frequencies (%) 1983-1996

Least Bittern
Ixobrychus exilis

Annual probability (%) of sighting this species in Wisconsin

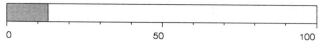

Average weekly reporting frequencies (%) by region

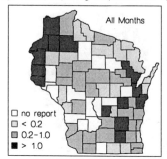

All Months

no report
< 0.2
0.2–1.0
> 1.0

Average weekly reporting frequencies (%) during year

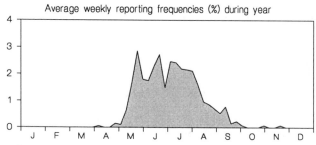

Changes in average weekly reporting frequencies (%) 1983–1996

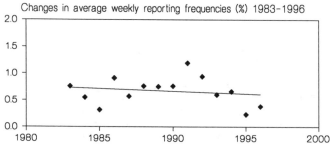

Great Blue Heron
Ardea herodias

Annual probability (%) of sighting this species in Wisconsin

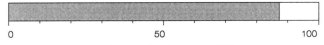

0　　　　　　　　　　　　　50　　　　　　　　　　　　100

Average weekly reporting frequencies (%) by region

All Months

☐ no report
☐ < 20.9
▨ 20.9-42.1
■ > 42.1

Average weekly reporting frequencies (%) during year

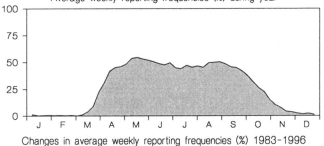

Changes in average weekly reporting frequencies (%) 1983-1996

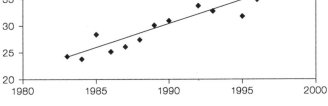

Great Egret
Ardea alba

Annual probability (%) of sighting this species in Wisconsin

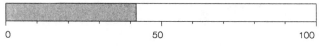

| 0 | 50 | 100 |

Average weekly reporting frequencies (%) by region

All Months

□ no report
□ < 0.9
▨ 0.9-8.5
■ > 8.5

Average weekly reporting frequencies (%) during year

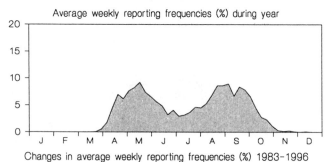

Changes in average weekly reporting frequencies (%) 1983-1996

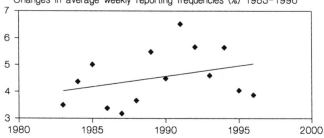

Cattle Egret
Bubulcus ibis

Annual probability (%) of sighting this species in Wisconsin

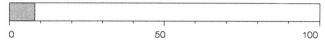

0   50   100

Average weekly reporting frequencies (%) by region

All Months

☐ no report
☐ < 0.1
▨ 0.1–0.4
■ > 0.4

Average weekly reporting frequencies (%) during year

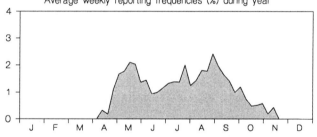

Changes in average weekly reporting frequencies (%) 1983–1996

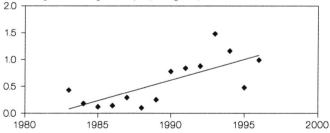

Green Heron
Butorides striatus

Annual probability (%) of sighting this species in Wisconsin

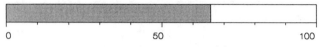

0	50	100

Average weekly reporting frequencies (%) by region

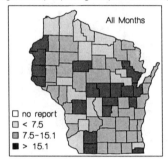

All Months

□ no report
□ < 7.5
▨ 7.5-15.1
■ > 15.1

Average weekly reporting frequencies (%) during year

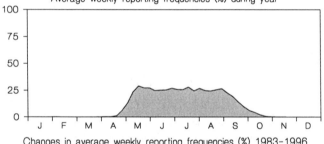

Changes in average weekly reporting frequencies (%) 1983-1996

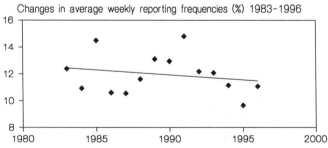

Black-crowned Night-heron
Nycticorax nycticorax

Annual probability (%) of sighting this species in Wisconsin

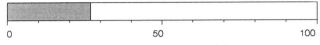

0	50	100

Average weekly reporting frequencies (%) by region

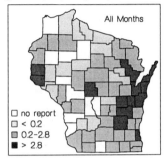

All Months

□ no report
□ < 0.2
▨ 0.2-2.8
■ > 2.8

Average weekly reporting frequencies (%) during year

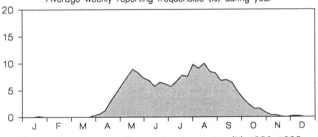

Changes in average weekly reporting frequencies (%) 1983-1996

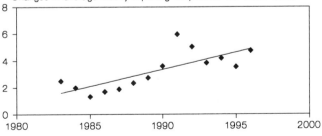

Yellow-crowned Night-heron
Nycticorax violaceus

Annual probability (%) of sighting this species in Wisconsin

0 50 100

Average weekly reporting frequencies (%) by region

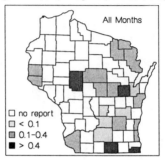

All Months

□ no report
□ < 0.1
▨ 0.1–0.4
■ > 0.4

Average weekly reporting frequencies (%) during year

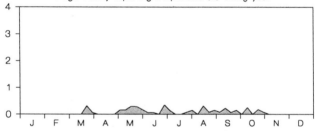

J F M A M J J A S O N D

Changes in average weekly reporting frequencies (%) 1983-1996

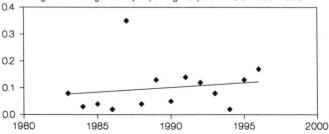

1980 1985 1990 1995 2000

Tundra Swan
Cygnus columbianus

Annual probability (%) of sighting this species in Wisconsin

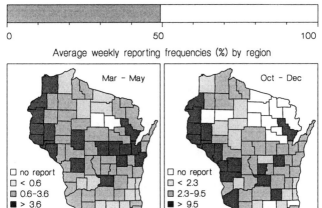

Average weekly reporting frequencies (%) by region

Mar – May	Oct – Dec

□ no report
□ < 0.6
▨ 0.6–3.6
■ > 3.6

□ no report
□ < 2.3
▨ 2.3–9.5
■ > 9.5

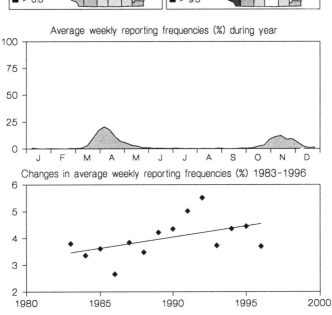

Average weekly reporting frequencies (%) during year

Changes in average weekly reporting frequencies (%) 1983–1996

Mute Swan
Cygnus olor

Annual probability (%) of sighting this species in Wisconsin

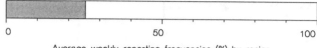

0   50   100

Average weekly reporting frequencies (%) by region

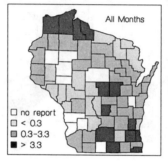

All Months

□ no report
□ < 0.3
▨ 0.3–3.3
■ > 3.3

Average weekly reporting frequencies (%) during year

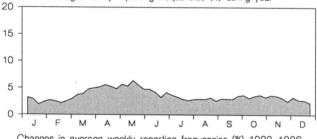

Changes in average weekly reporting frequencies (%) 1983–1996

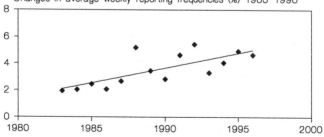

Snow Goose
Chen caerulescens

Annual probability (%) of sighting this species in Wisconsin

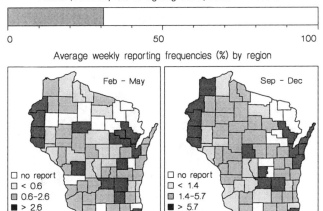

Average weekly reporting frequencies (%) by region

Feb – May

Sep – Dec

□ no report
□ < 0.6
▨ 0.6-2.6
■ > 2.6

□ no report
□ < 1.4
▨ 1.4-5.7
■ > 5.7

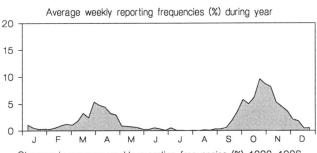

Average weekly reporting frequencies (%) during year

J F M A M J J A S O N D

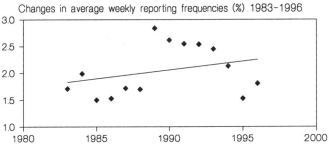

Changes in average weekly reporting frequencies (%) 1983-1996

Canada Goose
Branta canadensis

Annual probability (%) of sighting this species in Wisconsin

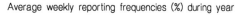

0   50   100

Average weekly reporting frequencies (%) by region

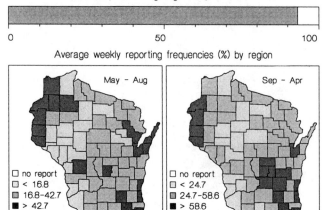

May – Aug

□ no report
□ < 16.8
▨ 16.8–42.7
■ > 42.7

Sep – Apr

□ no report
□ < 24.7
▨ 24.7–58.6
■ > 58.6

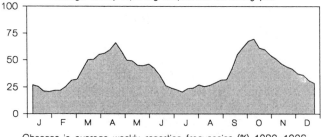

Average weekly reporting frequencies (%) during year

Changes in average weekly reporting frequencies (%) 1983–1996

Wood Duck
Aix sponsa

Annual probability (%) of sighting this species in Wisconsin

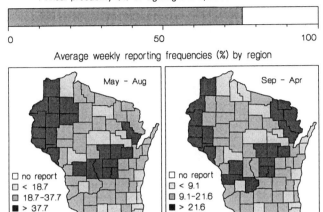

Average weekly reporting frequencies (%) by region

May – Aug

Sep – Apr

□ no report
□ < 18.7
▨ 18.7-37.7
■ > 37.7

□ no report
□ < 9.1
▨ 9.1-21.6
■ > 21.6

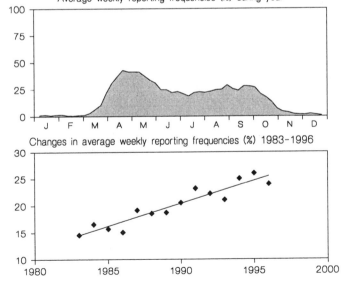

Average weekly reporting frequencies (%) during year

Changes in average weekly reporting frequencies (%) 1983-1996

Green-winged Teal
Anas crecca

Annual probability (%) of sighting this species in Wisconsin

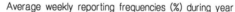

0   50   100

Average weekly reporting frequencies (%) by region

All Months

- □ no report
- □ < 1.5
- ▨ 1.5-7.0
- ■ > 7.0

Average weekly reporting frequencies (%) during year

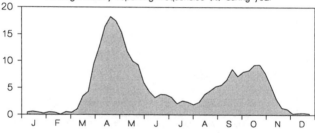

Changes in average weekly reporting frequencies (%) 1983-1996

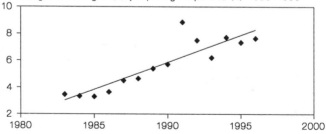

American Black Duck
Anas rubripes

Annual probability (%) of sighting this species in Wisconsin

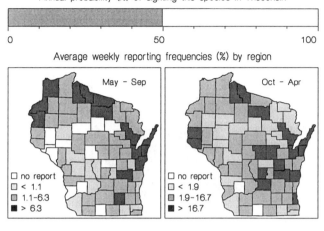

Average weekly reporting frequencies (%) by region

Average weekly reporting frequencies (%) during year

Changes in average weekly reporting frequencies (%) 1983-1996

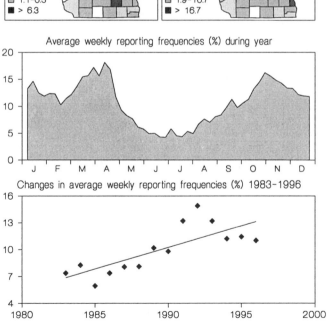

Mallard
Anas platyrhynchos

Annual probability (%) of sighting this species in Wisconsin

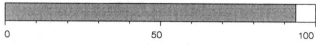

| 0 | 50 | 100 |

Average weekly reporting frequencies (%) by region

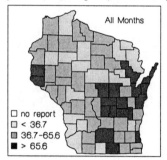

All Months

- □ no report
- □ < 36.7
- ▩ 36.7–65.6
- ■ > 65.6

Average weekly reporting frequencies (%) during year

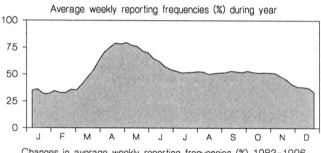

Changes in average weekly reporting frequencies (%) 1983–1996

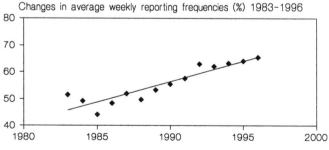

Northern Pintail
Anas acuta

Annual probability (%) of sighting this species in Wisconsin

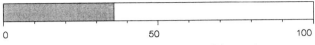

Average weekly reporting frequencies (%) by region

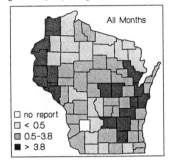

All Months

□ no report
□ < 0.5
▨ 0.5-3.8
■ > 3.8

Average weekly reporting frequencies (%) during year

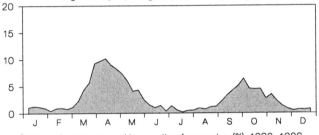

Changes in average weekly reporting frequencies (%) 1983-1996

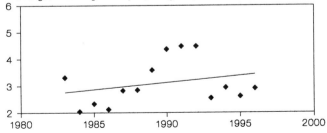

Blue-winged Teal
Anas discors

Annual probability (%) of sighting this species in Wisconsin

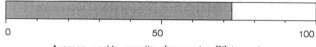

0	50	100

Average weekly reporting frequencies (%) by region

All Months

□ no report
□ < 10.0
▨ 10.0-22.6
■ > 22.6

Average weekly reporting frequencies (%) during year

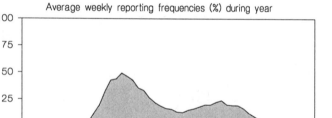

Changes in average weekly reporting frequencies (%) 1983-1996

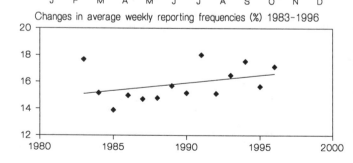

Northern Shoveler
Anas clypeata

Annual probability (%) of sighting this species in Wisconsin

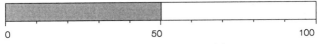

0	50	100

Average weekly reporting frequencies (%) by region

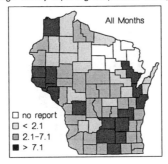

All Months

□ no report
□ < 2.1
▨ 2.1–7.1
■ > 7.1

Average weekly reporting frequencies (%) during year

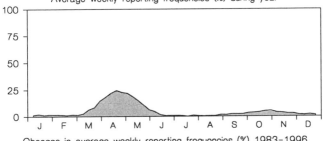

Changes in average weekly reporting frequencies (%) 1983–1996

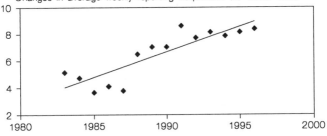

Gadwall
Anas strepera

Annual probability (%) of sighting this species in Wisconsin

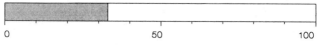

| 0 | 50 | 100 |

Average weekly reporting frequencies (%) by region

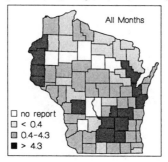

All Months

□ no report
□ < 0.4
▨ 0.4-4.3
■ > 4.3

Average weekly reporting frequencies (%) during year

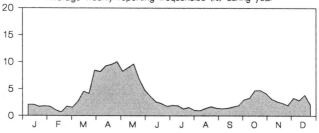

Changes in average weekly reporting frequencies (%) 1983-1996

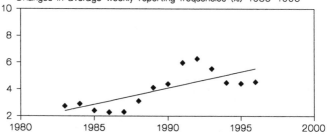

American Wigeon
Anas americana

Annual probability (%) of sighting this species in Wisconsin

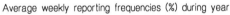

0	50	100

Average weekly reporting frequencies (%) by region

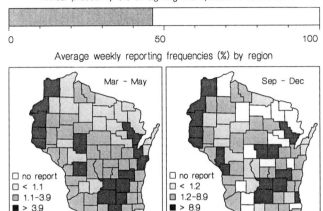

Mar – May

□ no report
□ < 1.1
▨ 1.1-3.9
■ > 3.9

Sep – Dec

□ no report
□ < 1.2
▨ 1.2-8.9
■ > 8.9

Average weekly reporting frequencies (%) during year

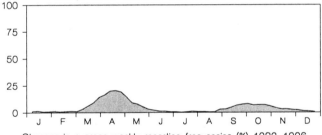

Changes in average weekly reporting frequencies (%) 1983-1996

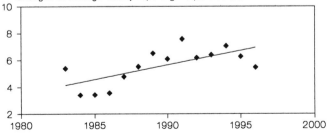

Canvasback
Aythya valisineria

Annual probability (%) of sighting this species in Wisconsin

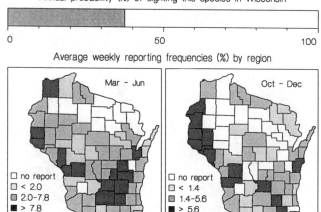

Average weekly reporting frequencies (%) by region

Average weekly reporting frequencies (%) during year

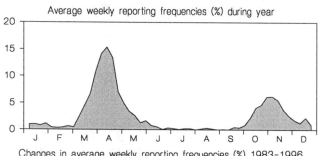

Changes in average weekly reporting frequencies (%) 1983-1996

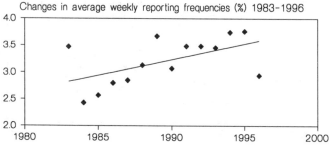

Redhead
Aythya americana

Annual probability (%) of sighting this species in Wisconsin

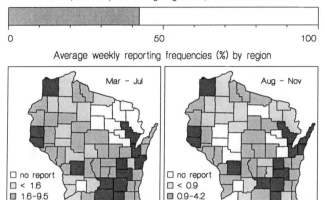

Average weekly reporting frequencies (%) by region

Mar – Jul

Aug – Nov

☐ no report
☐ < 1.6
▦ 1.6-9.5
■ > 9.5

☐ no report
☐ < 0.9
▦ 0.9-4.2
■ > 4.2

Average weekly reporting frequencies (%) during year

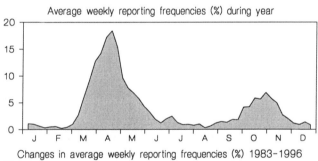

Changes in average weekly reporting frequencies (%) 1983-1996

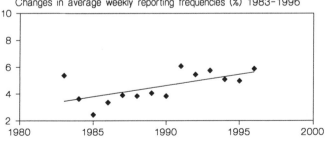

Ring-necked Duck
Aythya collaris

Annual probability (%) of sighting this species in Wisconsin

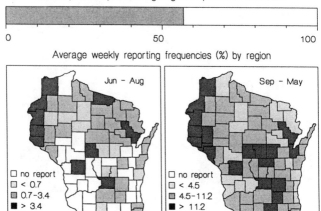

Average weekly reporting frequencies (%) by region

Jun – Aug

☐ no report
☐ < 0.7
▨ 0.7-3.4
■ > 3.4

Sep – May

☐ no report
☐ < 4.5
▨ 4.5-11.2
■ > 11.2

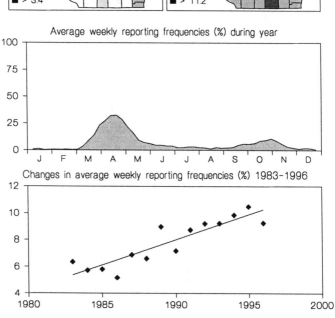

Average weekly reporting frequencies (%) during year

Changes in average weekly reporting frequencies (%) 1983-1996

Greater Scaup
Aythya marila

Annual probability (%) of sighting this species in Wisconsin

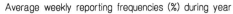

0   50   100

Average weekly reporting frequencies (%) by region

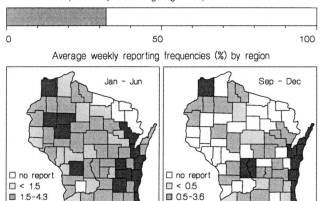

Jan – Jun

Sep – Dec

□ no report
□ < 1.5
▨ 1.5–4.3
■ > 4.3

□ no report
□ < 0.5
▨ 0.5–3.6
■ > 3.6

Average weekly reporting frequencies (%) during year

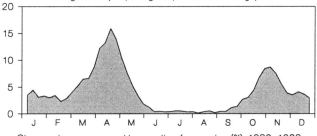

Changes in average weekly reporting frequencies (%) 1983–1996

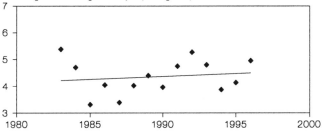

Lesser Scaup
Aythya affinis

Annual probability (%) of sighting this species in Wisconsin

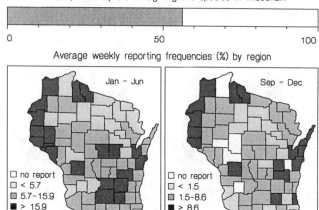

Average weekly reporting frequencies (%) by region

Jan – Jun
Sep – Dec

□ no report
□ < 5.7
▨ 5.7–15.9
■ > 15.9

□ no report
□ < 1.5
▨ 1.5–8.6
■ > 8.6

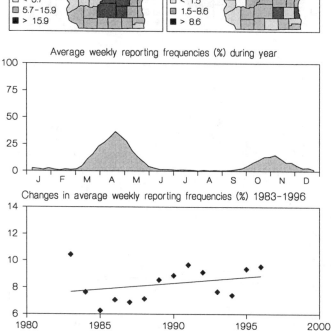

Average weekly reporting frequencies (%) during year

Changes in average weekly reporting frequencies (%) 1983–1996

Oldsquaw
Clangula hyemalis

Annual probability (%) of sighting this species in Wisconsin

| 0 | 50 | 100 |

Average weekly reporting frequencies (%) by region

All Months

- □ no report
- □ < 0.1
- ▨ 0.1–0.3
- ■ > 0.3

Average weekly reporting frequencies (%) during year

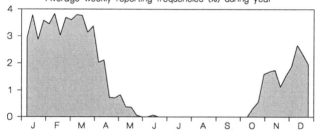

Changes in average weekly reporting frequencies (%) 1983–1996

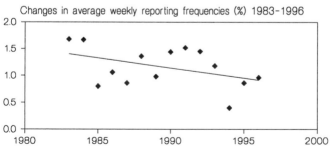

Black Scoter
Melanitta nigra

Annual probability (%) of sighting this species in Wisconsin

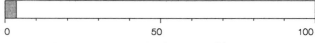

0   50   100

Average weekly reporting frequencies (%) by region

All Months

□ no report
□ < 0.1
▨ 0.1–0.7
■ > 0.7

Average weekly reporting frequencies (%) during year

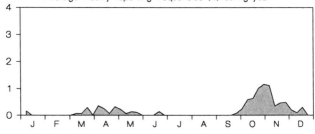

J F M A M J J A S O N D

Changes in average weekly reporting frequencies (%) 1983–1996

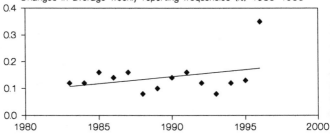

Surf Scoter
Melanitta perspicillata

Annual probability (%) of sighting this species in Wisconsin

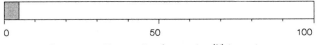

0   50   100

Average weekly reporting frequencies (%) by region

All Months

□ no report
□ < 0.1
▨ 0.1–0.8
■ > 0.8

Average weekly reporting frequencies (%) during year

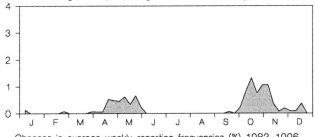

J F M A M J J A S O N D

Changes in average weekly reporting frequencies (%) 1983–1996

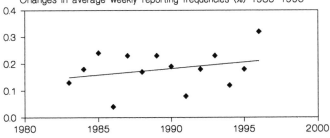

White-winged Scoter
Melanitta fusca

Annual probability (%) of sighting this species in Wisconsin

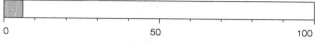

| 0 | 50 | 100 |

Average weekly reporting frequencies (%) by region

All Months

□ no report
□ < 0.1
▧ 0.1–0.5
■ > 0.5

Average weekly reporting frequencies (%) during year

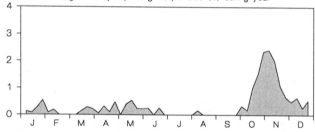

Changes in average weekly reporting frequencies (%) 1983–1996

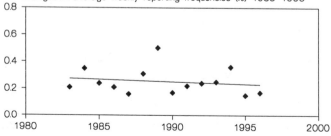

Common Goldeneye
Bucephala clangula

Annual probability (%) of sighting this species in Wisconsin

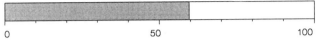

| 0 | 50 | 100 |

Average weekly reporting frequencies (%) by region

All Months

☐ no report
☐ < 3.7
▨ 3.7-13.4
■ > 13.4

Average weekly reporting frequencies (%) during year

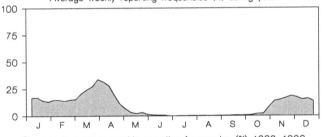

Changes in average weekly reporting frequencies (%) 1983-1996

Bufflehead
Bucephala albeola

Annual probability (%) of sighting this species in Wisconsin

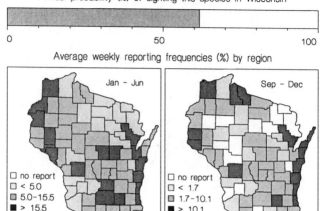

Average weekly reporting frequencies (%) by region

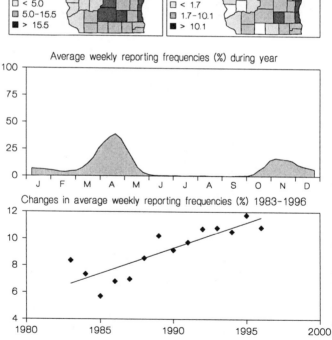

Hooded Merganser
Lophodytes cucullatus

Annual probability (%) of sighting this species in Wisconsin

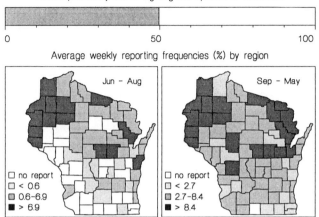

0   50   100

Average weekly reporting frequencies (%) by region

Jun – Aug

Sep – May

□ no report
□ < 0.6
▨ 0.6-6.9
■ > 6.9

□ no report
□ < 2.7
▨ 2.7-8.4
■ > 8.4

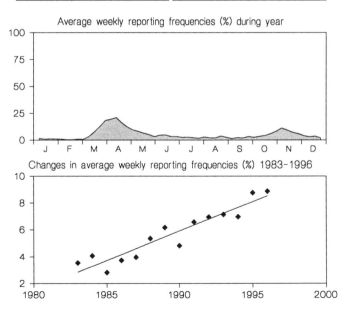

Average weekly reporting frequencies (%) during year

100
75
50
25
0
J   F   M   A   M   J   J   A   S   O   N   D

Changes in average weekly reporting frequencies (%) 1983-1996

10
8
6
4
2
1980   1985   1990   1995   2000

Common Merganser
Mergus merganser

Annual probability (%) of sighting this species in Wisconsin

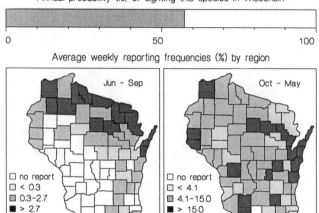

Average weekly reporting frequencies (%) by region

Average weekly reporting frequencies (%) during year

Changes in average weekly reporting frequencies (%) 1983–1996

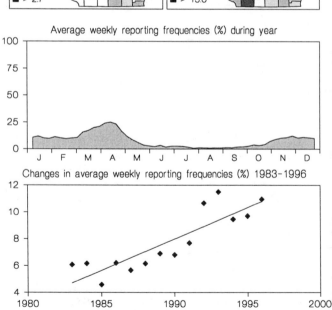

Red-breasted Merganser
Mergus serrator

Annual probability (%) of sighting this species in Wisconsin

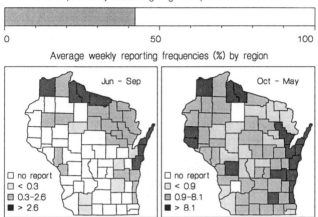

Average weekly reporting frequencies (%) by region

Jun – Sep

Oct – May

- □ no report
- □ < 0.3
- ▨ 0.3-2.6
- ■ > 2.6

- □ no report
- □ < 0.9
- ▨ 0.9-8.1
- ■ > 8.1

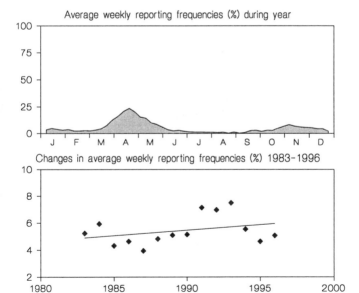

Average weekly reporting frequencies (%) during year

Changes in average weekly reporting frequencies (%) 1983-1996

Ruddy Duck
Oxyura jamaicensis

Annual probability (%) of sighting this species in Wisconsin

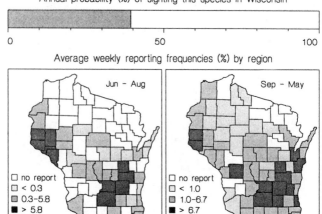

Average weekly reporting frequencies (%) by region

Jun – Aug

□ no report
□ < 0.3
▨ 0.3–5.8
■ > 5.8

Sep – May

□ no report
□ < 1.0
▨ 1.0–6.7
■ > 6.7

Average weekly reporting frequencies (%) during year

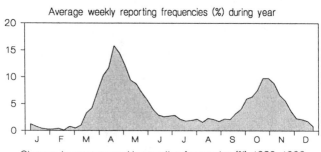

J F M A M J J A S O N D

Changes in average weekly reporting frequencies (%) 1983–1996

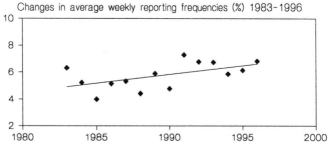

Turkey Vulture
Cathartes aura

Annual probability (%) of sighting this species in Wisconsin

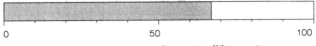

| 0 | 50 | 100 |

Average weekly reporting frequencies (%) by region

All Months

□ no report
□ < 5.6
▨ 5.6-20.8
■ > 20.8

Average weekly reporting frequencies (%) during year

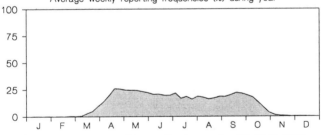

Changes in average weekly reporting frequencies (%) 1983-1996

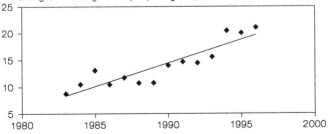

Osprey
Pandion haliaetus

Annual probability (%) of sighting this species in Wisconsin

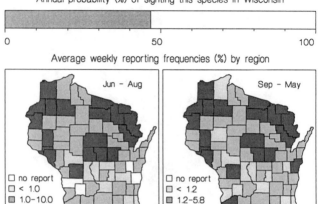

Average weekly reporting frequencies (%) by region

Jun – Aug

☐ no report
☐ < 1.0
▨ 1.0-10.0
■ > 10.0

Sep – May

☐ no report
☐ < 1.2
▨ 1.2-5.8
■ > 5.8

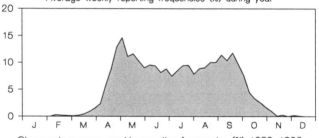

Average weekly reporting frequencies (%) during year

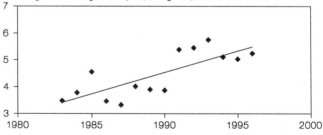

Changes in average weekly reporting frequencies (%) 1983-1996

Bald Eagle
Haliaeetus leucocephalus

Annual probability (%) of sighting this species in Wisconsin

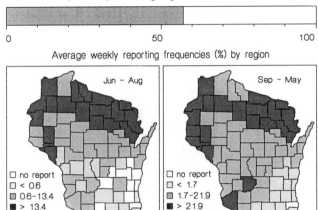

Average weekly reporting frequencies (%) by region

Jun – Aug

☐ no report
☐ < 0.6
▨ 0.6–13.4
■ > 13.4

Sep – May

☐ no report
☐ < 1.7
▨ 1.7–21.9
■ > 21.9

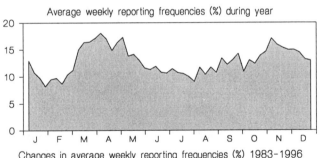

Average weekly reporting frequencies (%) during year

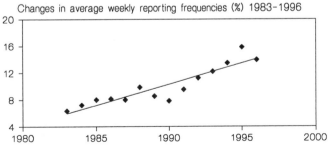

Changes in average weekly reporting frequencies (%) 1983–1996

Northern Harrier
Circus cyaneus

Annual probability (%) of sighting this species in Wisconsin

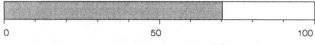

0   50   100

Average weekly reporting frequencies (%) by region

All Months

☐ no report
☐ < 7.4
▨ 7.4–22.6
■ > 22.6

Average weekly reporting frequencies (%) during year

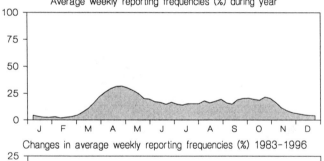

Changes in average weekly reporting frequencies (%) 1983–1996

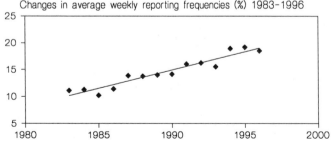

Sharp-shinned Hawk
Accipiter striatus

Annual probability (%) of sighting this species in Wisconsin

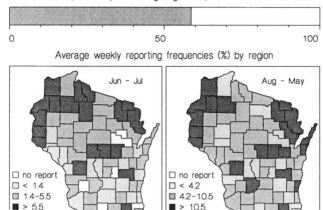

Average weekly reporting frequencies (%) by region

Jun – Jul

Aug – May

□ no report
□ < 1.4
▨ 1.4–5.5
■ > 5.5

□ no report
□ < 4.2
▨ 4.2–10.5
■ > 10.5

Average weekly reporting frequencies (%) during year

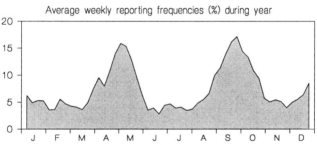

Changes in average weekly reporting frequencies (%) 1983–1996

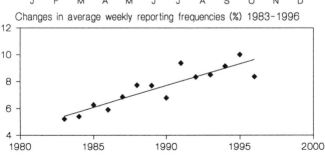

Cooper's Hawk
Accipiter cooperii

Annual probability (%) of sighting this species in Wisconsin

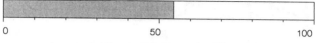

| 0 | 50 | 100 |

Average weekly reporting frequencies (%) by region

All Months

☐ no report
☐ < 2.7
▨ 2.7-9.3
■ > 9.3

Average weekly reporting frequencies (%) during year

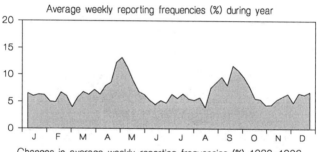

Changes in average weekly reporting frequencies (%) 1983-1996

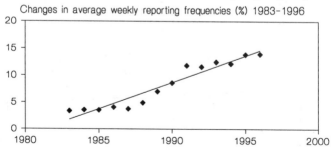

Northern Goshawk
Accipiter gentilis

Annual probability (%) of sighting this species in Wisconsin

0	50	100

Average weekly reporting frequencies (%) by region

All Months

□ no report
▨ < 0.6
▨ 0.6-2.7
■ > 2.7

Average weekly reporting frequencies (%) during year

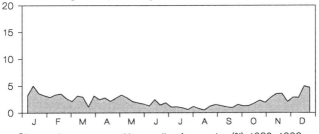

Changes in average weekly reporting frequencies (%) 1983-1996

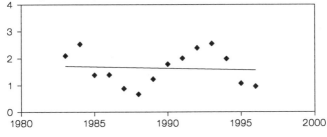

Red-shouldered Hawk
Buteo lineatus

Annual probability (%) of sighting this species in Wisconsin

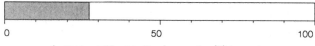

| 0 | 50 | 100 |

Average weekly reporting frequencies (%) by region

All Months

☐ no report
☐ < 0.6
▦ 0.6-3.3
■ > 3.3

Average weekly reporting frequencies (%) during year

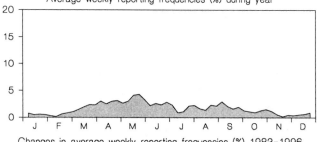

Changes in average weekly reporting frequencies (%) 1983-1996

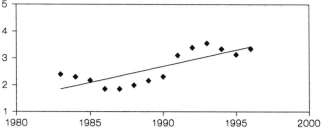

Broad-winged Hawk
Buteo platypterus

Annual probability (%) of sighting this species in Wisconsin

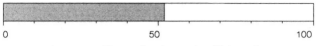

0	50	100

Average weekly reporting frequencies (%) by region

All Months

□ no report
□ < 2.2
▨ 2.2-9.2
■ > 9.2

Average weekly reporting frequencies (%) during year

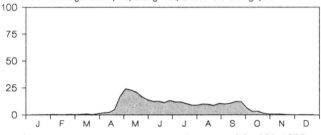

Changes in average weekly reporting frequencies (%) 1983-1996

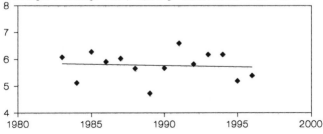

81

Red-tailed Hawk
Buteo jamaicensis

Annual probability (%) of sighting this species in Wisconsin

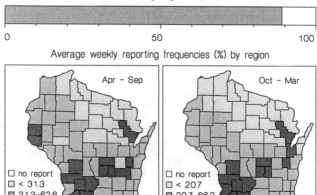

| 0 | 50 | 100 |

Average weekly reporting frequencies (%) by region

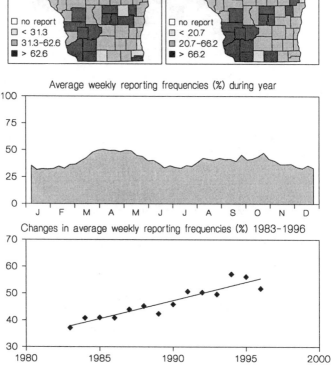

Apr – Sep

Oct – Mar

□ no report
□ < 31.3
▨ 31.3-62.6
■ > 62.6

□ no report
□ < 20.7
▨ 20.7-66.2
■ > 66.2

Average weekly reporting frequencies (%) during year

J F M A M J J A S O N D

Changes in average weekly reporting frequencies (%) 1983-1996

Rough-legged Hawk
Buteo lagopus

Annual probability (%) of sighting this species in Wisconsin

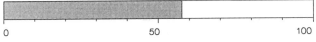

0   50   100

Average weekly reporting frequencies (%) by region

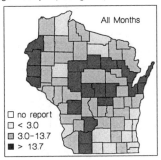

All Months

- □ no report
- □ < 3.0
- ▨ 3.0-13.7
- ■ > 13.7

Average weekly reporting frequencies (%) during year

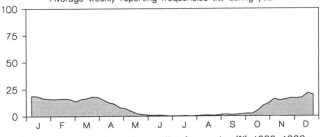

Changes in average weekly reporting frequencies (%) 1983-1996

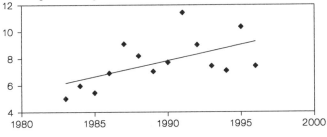

American Kestrel
Falco sparverius

Annual probability (%) of sighting this species in Wisconsin

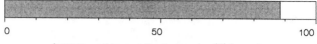

Average weekly reporting frequencies (%) by region

Average weekly reporting frequencies (%) during year

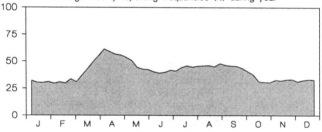

Changes in average weekly reporting frequencies (%) 1983-1996

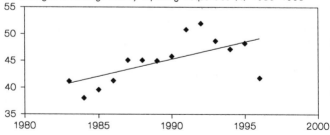

Merlin
Falco columbarius

Annual probability (%) of sighting this species in Wisconsin

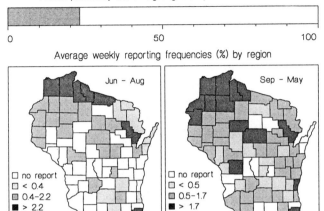

Average weekly reporting frequencies (%) by region

Jun – Aug

Sep – May

□ no report
□ < 0.4
▨ 0.4–2.2
■ > 2.2

□ no report
□ < 0.5
▨ 0.5–1.7
■ > 1.7

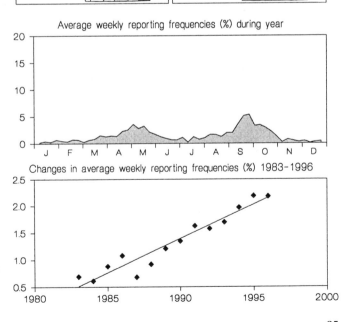

Average weekly reporting frequencies (%) during year

Changes in average weekly reporting frequencies (%) 1983–1996

Peregrine Falcon
Falco peregrinus

Annual probability (%) of sighting this species in Wisconsin

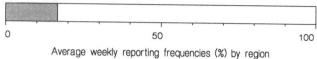

Average weekly reporting frequencies (%) by region

Average weekly reporting frequencies (%) during year

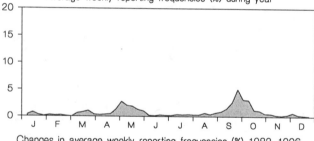

Changes in average weekly reporting frequencies (%) 1983–1996

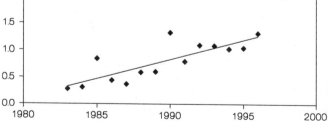

Gray Partridge
Perdix perdix

Annual probability (%) of sighting this species in Wisconsin

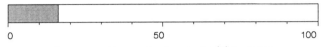

| 0 | 50 | 100 |

Average weekly reporting frequencies (%) by region

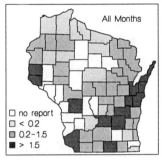

All Months

no report
< 0.2
0.2-1.5
> 1.5

Average weekly reporting frequencies (%) during year

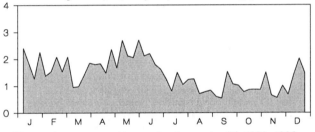

Changes in average weekly reporting frequencies (%) 1983-1996

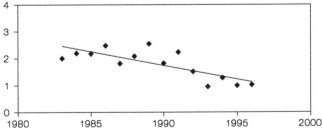

Ring-necked Pheasant
Phasianus colchicus

Annual probability (%) of sighting this species in Wisconsin

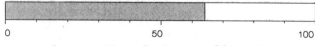

0   50   100

Average weekly reporting frequencies (%) by region

All Months

no report
< 3.5
3.5–20.6
> 20.6

Average weekly reporting frequencies (%) during year

Changes in average weekly reporting frequencies (%) 1983–1996

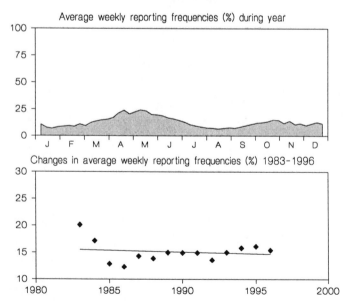

Ruffed Grouse
Bonasa umbellus

Annual probability (%) of sighting this species in Wisconsin

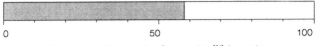

0 50 100

Average weekly reporting frequencies (%) by region

All Months

□ no report
□ < 5.1
▨ 5.1-29.9
■ > 29.9

Average weekly reporting frequencies (%) during year

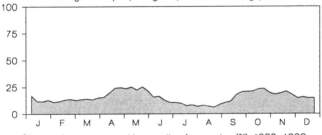

Changes in average weekly reporting frequencies (%) 1983-1996

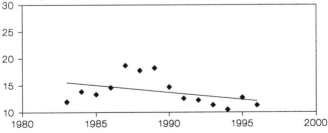

Greater Prairie-chicken
Tympanuchus cupido

Annual probability (%) of sighting this species in Wisconsin

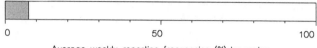

| 0 | 50 | 100 |

Average weekly reporting frequencies (%) by region

All Months

□ no report
□ < 0.2
▨ 0.2-9.9
■ > 9.9

Average weekly reporting frequencies (%) during year

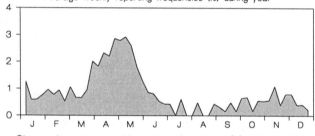

Changes in average weekly reporting frequencies (%) 1983-1996

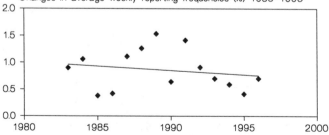

Sharp-tailed Grouse
Tympanuchus phasianellus

Annual probability (%) of sighting this species in Wisconsin

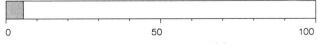

0   50   100

Average weekly reporting frequencies (%) by region

All Months

☐ no report
☐ < 0.1
▨ 0.1-0.9
■ > 0.9

Average weekly reporting frequencies (%) during year

Changes in average weekly reporting frequencies (%) 1983-1996

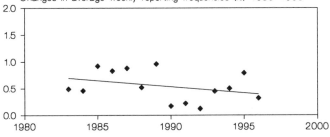

Wild Turkey
Meleagris gallopavo

Annual probability (%) of sighting this species in Wisconsin

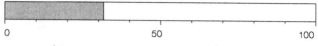

0	50	100

Average weekly reporting frequencies (%) by region

All Months

- □ no report
- □ < 0.8
- ▨ 0.8–8.0
- ■ > 8.0

Average weekly reporting frequencies (%) during year

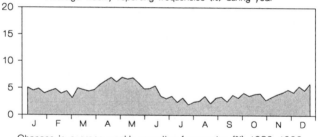

Changes in average weekly reporting frequencies (%) 1983–1996

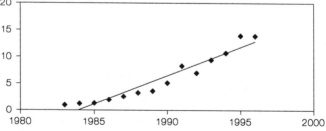

Northern Bobwhite
Colinus virginianus

Annual probability (%) of sighting this species in Wisconsin

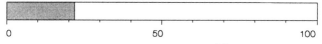

0   50   100

Average weekly reporting frequencies (%) by region

All Months

☐ no report
☐ < 0.3
▨ 0.3-3.0
■ > 3.0

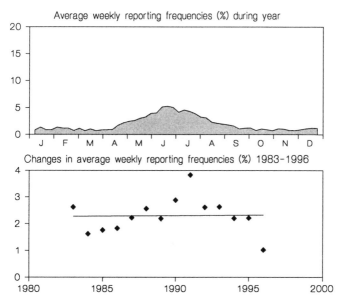

Average weekly reporting frequencies (%) during year

J F M A M J J A S O N D

Changes in average weekly reporting frequencies (%) 1983-1996

1980   1985   1990   1995   2000

Virginia Rail
Rallus limicola

Annual probability (%) of sighting this species in Wisconsin

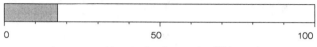

0	50	100

Average weekly reporting frequencies (%) by region

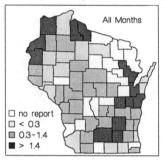

All Months

- ☐ no report
- ☐ < 0.3
- ▨ 0.3–1.4
- ■ > 1.4

Average weekly reporting frequencies (%) during year

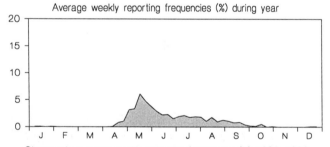

Changes in average weekly reporting frequencies (%) 1983–1996

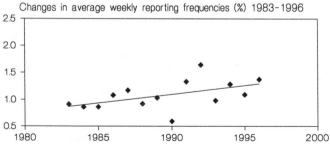

Sora
Porzana carolina

Annual probability (%) of sighting this species in Wisconsin

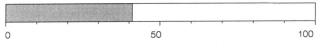

| 0 | 50 | 100 |

Average weekly reporting frequencies (%) by region

All Months

- □ no report
- □ < 1.1
- ▨ 1.1-5.7
- ■ > 5.7

Average weekly reporting frequencies (%) during year

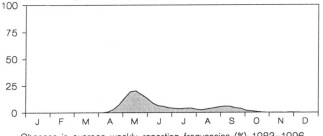

Changes in average weekly reporting frequencies (%) 1983-1996

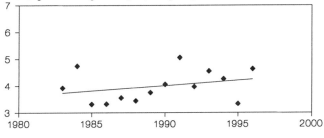

Common Moorhen
Gallinula chloropus

Annual probability (%) of sighting this species in Wisconsin

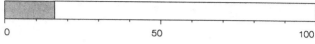

0 50 100

Average weekly reporting frequencies (%) by region

All Months

- □ no report
- □ < 0.2
- ▨ 0.2–1.7
- ■ > 1.7

Average weekly reporting frequencies (%) during year

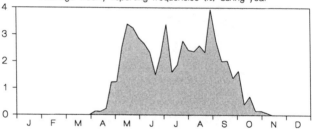

J F M A M J J A S O N D

Changes in average weekly reporting frequencies (%) 1983–1996

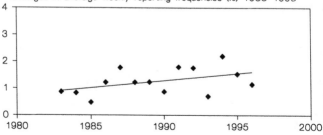

1980 1985 1990 1995 2000

American Coot
Fulica americana

Annual probability (%) of sighting this species in Wisconsin

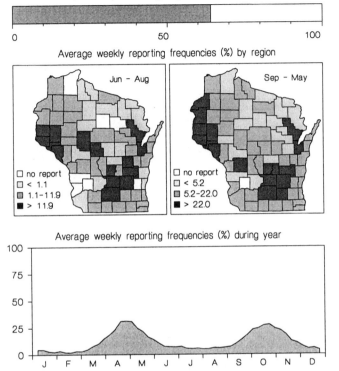

Average weekly reporting frequencies (%) by region

Jun – Aug

□ no report
□ < 1.1
▨ 1.1–11.9
■ > 11.9

Sep – May

□ no report
□ < 5.2
▨ 5.2–22.0
■ > 22.0

Average weekly reporting frequencies (%) during year

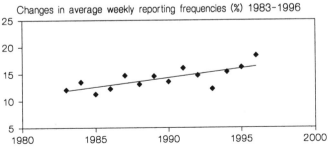

Changes in average weekly reporting frequencies (%) 1983–1996

Sandhill Crane
Grus canadensis

Annual probability (%) of sighting this species in Wisconsin

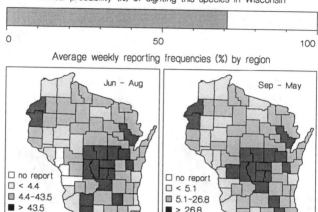

Average weekly reporting frequencies (%) by region

Jun – Aug

□ no report
□ < 4.4
▨ 4.4–43.5
■ > 43.5

Sep – May

□ no report
□ < 5.1
▨ 5.1–26.8
■ > 26.8

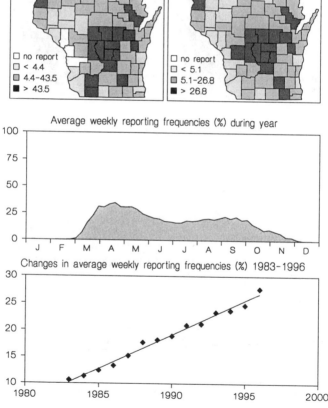

Average weekly reporting frequencies (%) during year

Changes in average weekly reporting frequencies (%) 1983–1996

Black-bellied Plover
Pluvialis squatarola

Annual probability (%) of sighting this species in Wisconsin

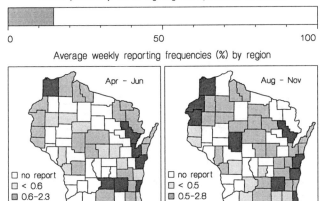

Average weekly reporting frequencies (%) by region

Apr – Jun

□ no report
□ < 0.6
▨ 0.6-2.3
■ > 2.3

Aug – Nov

□ no report
□ < 0.5
▨ 0.5-2.8
■ > 2.8

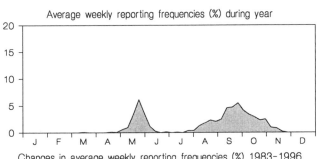

Average weekly reporting frequencies (%) during year

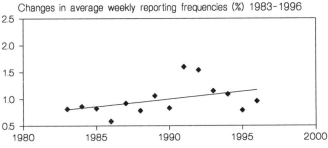

Changes in average weekly reporting frequencies (%) 1983-1996

American Golden-plover
Pluvialis dominicus

Annual probability (%) of sighting this species in Wisconsin

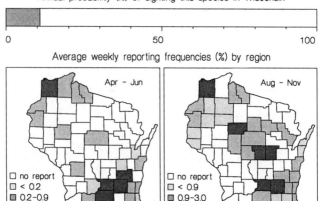

Average weekly reporting frequencies (%) by region

Apr – Jun

Aug – Nov

□ no report
□ < 0.2
▨ 0.2–0.9
■ > 0.9

□ no report
□ < 0.9
▨ 0.9–3.0
■ > 3.0

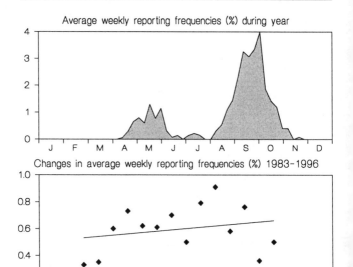

Average weekly reporting frequencies (%) during year

Changes in average weekly reporting frequencies (%) 1983-1996

Semipalmated Plover
Charadrius semipalmatus

Annual probability (%) of sighting this species in Wisconsin

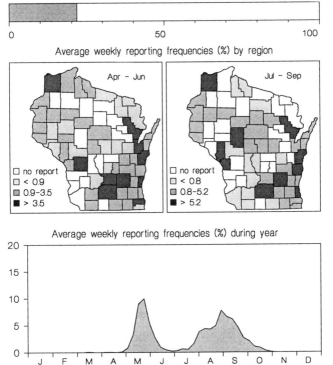

Average weekly reporting frequencies (%) by region

Apr – Jun

Jul – Sep

□ no report
□ < 0.9
▨ 0.9–3.5
■ > 3.5

□ no report
□ < 0.8
▨ 0.8–5.2
■ > 5.2

Average weekly reporting frequencies (%) during year

Changes in average weekly reporting frequencies (%) 1983–1996

Killdeer
Charadrius vociferus

Annual probability (%) of sighting this species in Wisconsin

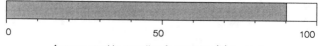

0	50	100

Average weekly reporting frequencies (%) by region

All Months

□ no report
□ < 34.2
▨ 34.2–49.4
■ > 49.4

Average weekly reporting frequencies (%) during year

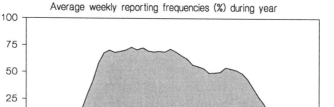

Changes in average weekly reporting frequencies (%) 1983–1996

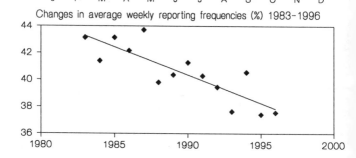

Greater Yellowlegs
Tringa melanoleuca

Annual probability (%) of sighting this species in Wisconsin

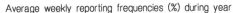

0   50   100

Average weekly reporting frequencies (%) by region

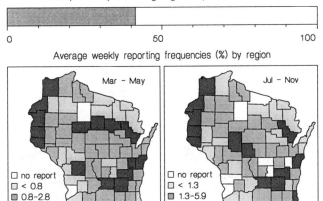

Mar – May

Jul – Nov

□ no report
□ < 0.8
▨ 0.8-2.8
■ > 2.8

□ no report
□ < 1.3
▨ 1.3-5.9
■ > 5.9

Average weekly reporting frequencies (%) during year

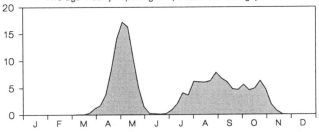

Changes in average weekly reporting frequencies (%) 1983-1996

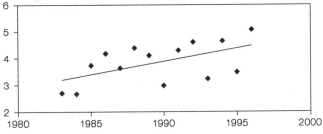

Lesser Yellowlegs
Tringa flavipes

Annual probability (%) of sighting this species in Wisconsin

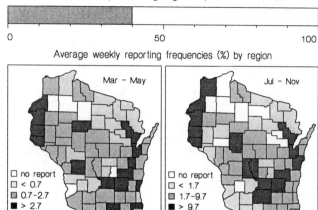

Average weekly reporting frequencies (%) by region

Mar – May

Jul – Nov

- □ no report
- □ < 0.7
- ▨ 0.7–2.7
- ■ > 2.7

- □ no report
- □ < 1.7
- ▨ 1.7–9.7
- ■ > 9.7

Average weekly reporting frequencies (%) during year

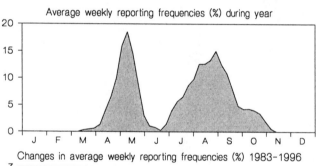

Changes in average weekly reporting frequencies (%) 1983–1996

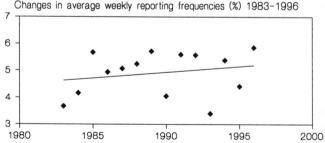

Solitary Sandpiper
Tringa solitaria

Annual probability (%) of sighting this species in Wisconsin

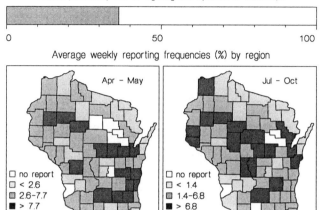

Average weekly reporting frequencies (%) by region

Apr – May

□ no report
□ < 2.6
▨ 2.6–7.7
■ > 7.7

Jul – Oct

□ no report
□ < 1.4
▨ 1.4–6.8
■ > 6.8

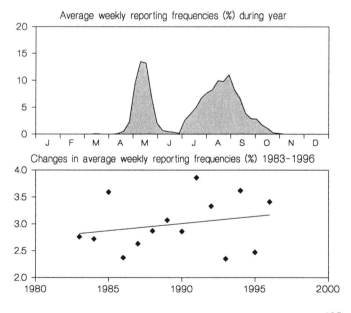

Average weekly reporting frequencies (%) during year

Changes in average weekly reporting frequencies (%) 1983–1996

Willet
Catoptrophorus semipalmatus

Annual probability (%) of sighting this species in Wisconsin

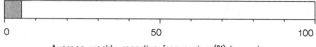

0	50	100

Average weekly reporting frequencies (%) by region

All Months

□ no report
▨ < 0.1
▨ 0.1-0.4
■ > 0.4

Average weekly reporting frequencies (%) during year

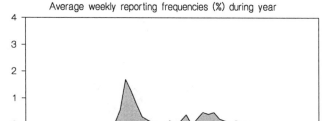

Changes in average weekly reporting frequencies (%) 1983-1996

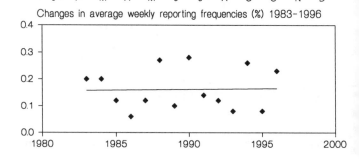

Spotted Sandpiper
Actitis macularia

Annual probability (%) of sighting this species in Wisconsin

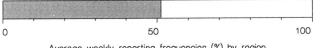

0   50   100

Average weekly reporting frequencies (%) by region

All Months

□ no report
□ < 3.5
▨ 3.5–8.2
■ > 8.2

Average weekly reporting frequencies (%) during year

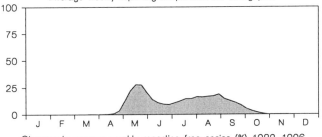

Changes in average weekly reporting frequencies (%) 1983–1996

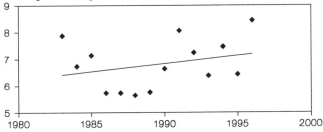

Upland Sandpiper
Bartramia longicauda

Annual probability (%) of sighting this species in Wisconsin

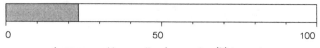

0   50   100

Average weekly reporting frequencies (%) by region

All Months

□ no report
▨ < 0.4
▨ 0.4-2.2
■ > 2.2

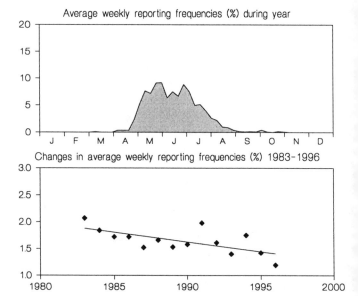

Average weekly reporting frequencies (%) during year

Changes in average weekly reporting frequencies (%) 1983-1996

Hudsonian Godwit
Limosa haemastica

Annual probability (%) of sighting this species in Wisconsin

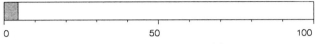

0   50   100

Average weekly reporting frequencies (%) by region

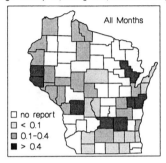

All Months

- □ no report
- ▨ < 0.1
- ▩ 0.1–0.4
- ■ > 0.4

Average weekly reporting frequencies (%) during year

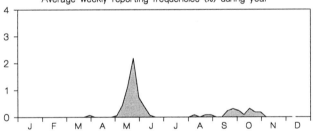

Changes in average weekly reporting frequencies (%) 1983–1996

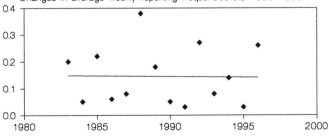

109

Marbled Godwit
Limosa fedoa

Annual probability (%) of sighting this species in Wisconsin

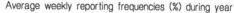

0   50   100

Average weekly reporting frequencies (%) by region

All Months

☐ no report
☐ < 0.1
▨ 0.1–0.4
■ > 0.4

Average weekly reporting frequencies (%) during year

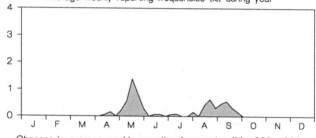

Changes in average weekly reporting frequencies (%) 1983–1996

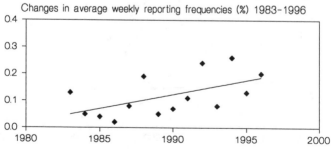

Ruddy Turnstone
Arenaria interpres

Annual probability (%) of sighting this species in Wisconsin

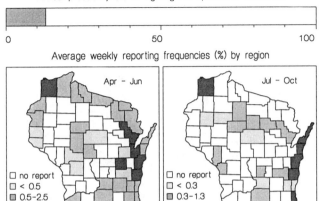

Average weekly reporting frequencies (%) by region

Apr – Jun

Jul – Oct

□ no report
□ < 0.5
▨ 0.5–2.5
■ > 2.5

□ no report
□ < 0.3
▨ 0.3–1.3
■ > 1.3

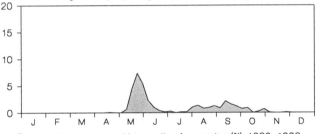

Average weekly reporting frequencies (%) during year

J F M A M J J A S O N D

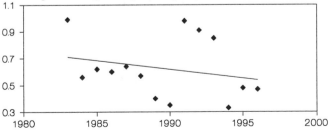

Changes in average weekly reporting frequencies (%) 1983–1996

Red Knot
Calidris canutus

Annual probability (%) of sighting this species in Wisconsin

0   50   100

Average weekly reporting frequencies (%) by region

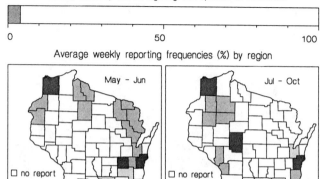

May – Jun

☐ no report
☐ < 0.5
▨ 0.5-1.8
■ > 1.8

Jul – Oct

☐ no report
☐ < 0.2
▨ 0.2-1.2
■ > 1.2

Average weekly reporting frequencies (%) during year

Changes in average weekly reporting frequencies (%) 1983-1996

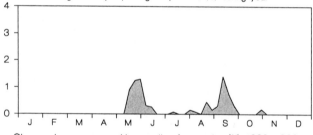

Sanderling
Calidris alba

Annual probability (%) of sighting this species in Wisconsin

0   50   100

Average weekly reporting frequencies (%) by region

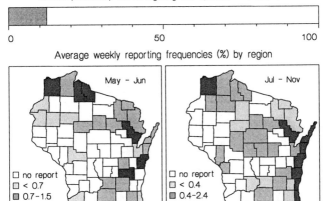

May – Jun

- ☐ no report
- ☐ < 0.7
- ☐ 0.7-1.5
- ■ > 1.5

Jul – Nov

- ☐ no report
- ☐ < 0.4
- ☐ 0.4-2.4
- ■ > 2.4

Average weekly reporting frequencies (%) during year

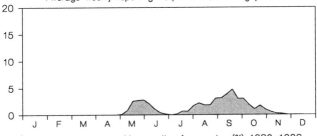

Changes in average weekly reporting frequencies (%) 1983-1996

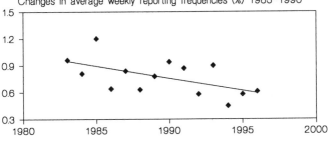

Semipalmated Sandpiper
Calidris pusilla

Annual probability (%) of sighting this species in Wisconsin

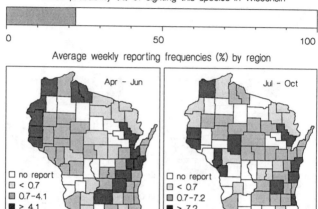

| 0 | 50 | 100 |

Average weekly reporting frequencies (%) by region

Apr – Jun

□ no report
□ < 0.7
▨ 0.7–4.1
■ > 4.1

Jul – Oct

□ no report
□ < 0.7
▨ 0.7–7.2
■ > 7.2

Average weekly reporting frequencies (%) during year

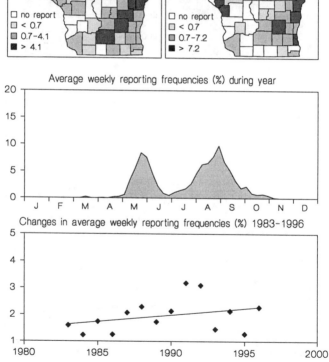

Changes in average weekly reporting frequencies (%) 1983-1996

Least Sandpiper
Calidris minutilla

Annual probability (%) of sighting this species in Wisconsin

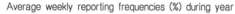

| 0 | 50 | 100 |

Average weekly reporting frequencies (%) by region

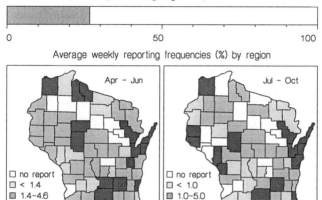

Apr – Jun

☐ no report
☐ < 1.4
▨ 1.4–4.6
■ > 4.6

Jul – Oct

☐ no report
☐ < 1.0
▨ 1.0–5.0
■ > 5.0

Average weekly reporting frequencies (%) during year

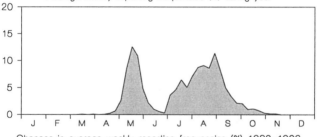

Changes in average weekly reporting frequencies (%) 1983–1996

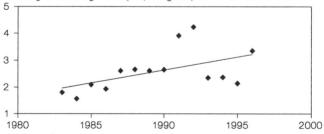

White-rumped Sandpiper
Calidris fuscicollis

Annual probability (%) of sighting this species in Wisconsin

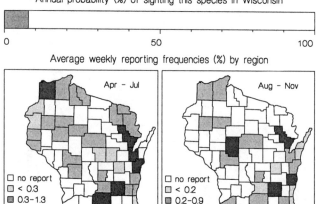

Average weekly reporting frequencies (%) by region

Apr – Jul

☐ no report
☐ < 0.3
▦ 0.3-1.3
■ > 1.3

Aug – Nov

☐ no report
☐ < 0.2
▦ 0.2-0.9
■ > 0.9

Average weekly reporting frequencies (%) during year

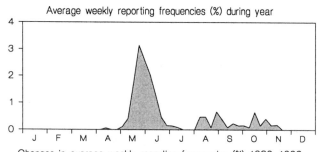

Changes in average weekly reporting frequencies (%) 1983-1996

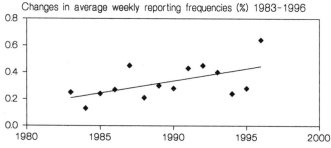

Baird's Sandpiper
Calidris bairdii

Annual probability (%) of sighting this species in Wisconsin

0   50   100

Average weekly reporting frequencies (%) by region

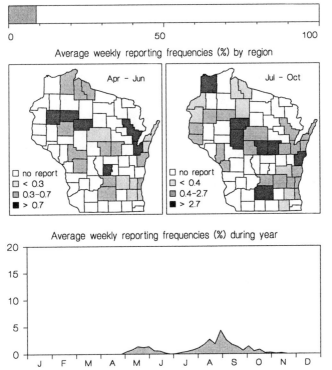

Average weekly reporting frequencies (%) during year

Changes in average weekly reporting frequencies (%) 1983-1996

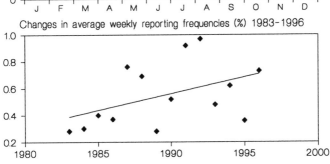

117

Pectoral Sandpiper
Calidris melanotos

Annual probability (%) of sighting this species in Wisconsin

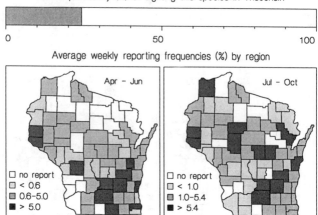

Average weekly reporting frequencies (%) by region

Apr – Jun

Jul – Oct

□ no report
□ < 0.6
▨ 0.6-5.0
■ > 5.0

□ no report
□ < 1.0
▨ 1.0-5.4
■ > 5.4

Average weekly reporting frequencies (%) during year

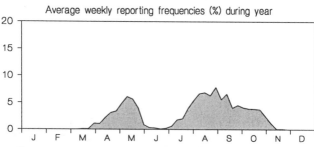

Changes in average weekly reporting frequencies (%) 1983-1996

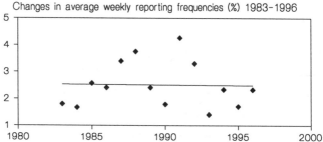

Dunlin
Calidris alpina

Annual probability (%) of sighting this species in Wisconsin

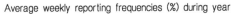

0   50   100

Average weekly reporting frequencies (%) by region

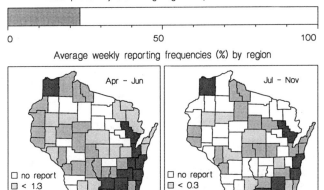

Apr – Jun

□ no report
□ < 1.3
▨ 1.3–5.4
■ > 5.4

Jul – Nov

□ no report
□ < 0.3
▨ 0.3–2.3
■ > 2.3

Average weekly reporting frequencies (%) during year

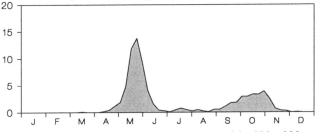

Changes in average weekly reporting frequencies (%) 1983–1996

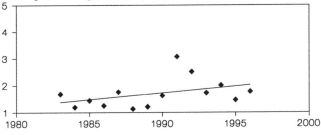

Stilt Sandpiper
Calidris himantopus

Annual probability (%) of sighting this species in Wisconsin

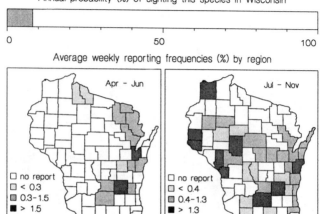

Average weekly reporting frequencies (%) by region

Apr – Jun

Jul – Nov

□ no report
□ < 0.3
▨ 0.3–1.5
■ > 1.5

□ no report
□ < 0.4
▨ 0.4–1.3
■ > 1.3

Average weekly reporting frequencies (%) during year

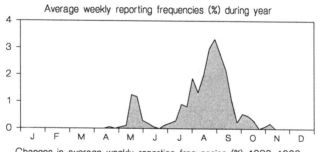

Changes in average weekly reporting frequencies (%) 1983–1996

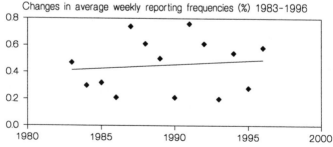

Short-billed Dowitcher
Limnodromus griseus

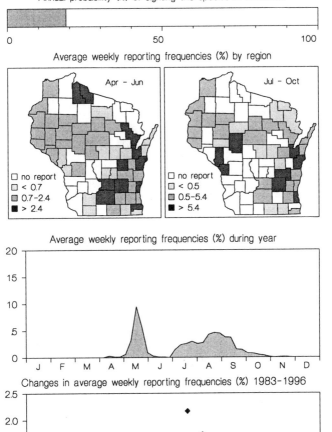

Annual probability (%) of sighting this species in Wisconsin

0   50   100

Average weekly reporting frequencies (%) by region

Apr – Jun

Jul – Oct

□ no report
□ < 0.7
▨ 0.7–2.4
■ > 2.4

□ no report
□ < 0.5
▨ 0.5–5.4
■ > 5.4

Average weekly reporting frequencies (%) during year

J F M A M J J A S O N D

Changes in average weekly reporting frequencies (%) 1983–1996

Long-billed Dowitcher
Limnodromus scolopaceus

Annual probability (%) of sighting this species in Wisconsin

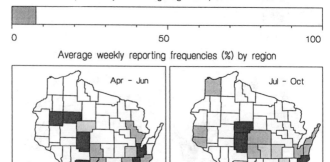

Average weekly reporting frequencies (%) by region

Apr – Jun

Jul – Oct

□ no report
□ < 0.4
▨ 0.4–1.0
■ > 1.0

□ no report
□ < 0.5
▨ 0.5–2.0
■ > 2.0

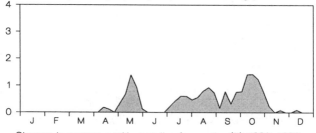

Average weekly reporting frequencies (%) during year

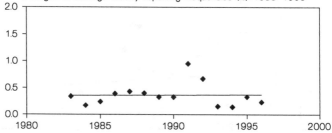

Changes in average weekly reporting frequencies (%) 1983-1996

Common Snipe
Gallinago gallinago

Annual probability (%) of sighting this species in Wisconsin

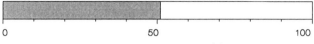

0   50   100

Average weekly reporting frequencies (%) by region

All Months

□ no report
□ < 2.7
▨ 2.7–8.1
■ > 8.1

Average weekly reporting frequencies (%) during year

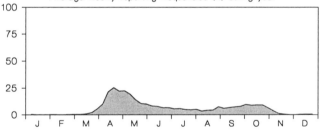

Changes in average weekly reporting frequencies (%) 1984–1996

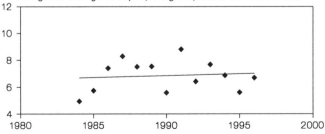

123

American Woodcock
Scolopax minor

Annual probability (%) of sighting this species in Wisconsin

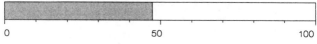

Average weekly reporting frequencies (%) by region

Average weekly reporting frequencies (%) during year

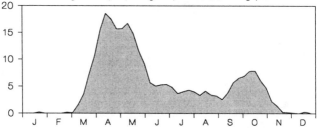

Changes in average weekly reporting frequencies (%) 1983-1996

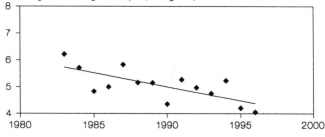

Wilson's Phalarope
Phalaropus tricolor

Annual probability (%) of sighting this species in Wisconsin

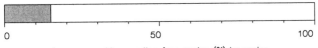

Average weekly reporting frequencies (%) by region

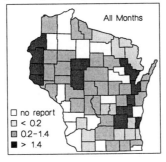

All Months

□ no report
□ < 0.2
▨ 0.2–1.4
■ > 1.4

Average weekly reporting frequencies (%) during year

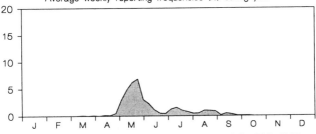

Changes in average weekly reporting frequencies (%) 1983–1996

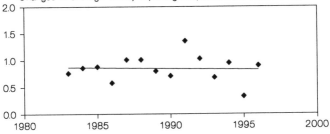

Red-necked Phalarope
Phalaropus lobatus

Annual probability (%) of sighting this species in Wisconsin

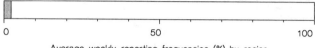

| 0 | 50 | 100 |

Average weekly reporting frequencies (%) by region

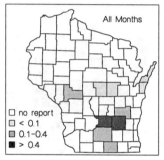

All Months

☐ no report
☐ < 0.1
▨ 0.1-0.4
■ > 0.4

Average weekly reporting frequencies (%) during year

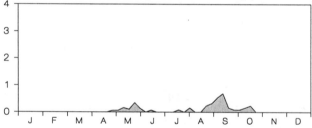

Changes in average weekly reporting frequencies (%) 1983-1996

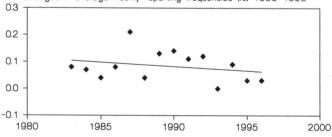

Franklin's Gull
Larus pipixcan

Annual probability (%) of sighting this species in Wisconsin

0   50   100

Average weekly reporting frequencies (%) by region

All Months

□ no report
□ < 0.1
▨ 0.1–0.4
■ > 0.4

Average weekly reporting frequencies (%) during year

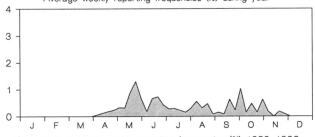

J F M A M J J A S O N D

Changes in average weekly reporting frequencies (%) 1983–1996

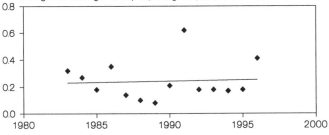

Bonaparte's Gull
Larus philadelphia

Annual probability (%) of sighting this species in Wisconsin

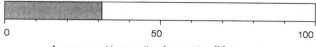

Average weekly reporting frequencies (%) by region

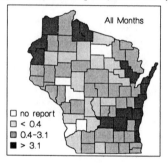

All Months

□ no report
▨ < 0.4
▨ 0.4-3.1
■ > 3.1

Average weekly reporting frequencies (%) during year

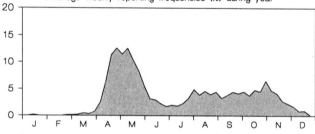

Changes in average weekly reporting frequencies (%) 1983-1996

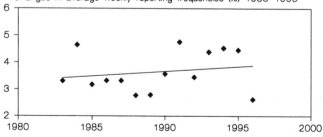

Ring-billed Gull
Larus delawarensis

Annual probability (%) of finding this species in Wisconsin

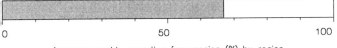

0   50   100

Average weekly reporting frequencies (%) by region

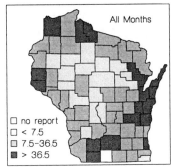

All Months

□ no report
□ < 7.5
▨ 7.5–36.5
■ > 36.5

Average weekly reporting frequencies (%) during year

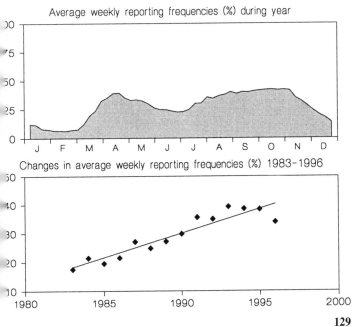

Changes in average weekly reporting frequencies (%) 1983–1996

Herring Gull
Larus argentatus

Annual probability (%) of sighting this species in Wisconsin

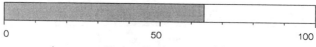

0	50	100

Average weekly reporting frequencies (%) by region

All Months

□ no report
□ < 4.4
▨ 4.4–23.4
■ > 23.4

Average weekly reporting frequencies (%) during year

Changes in average weekly reporting frequencies (%) 1983–1996

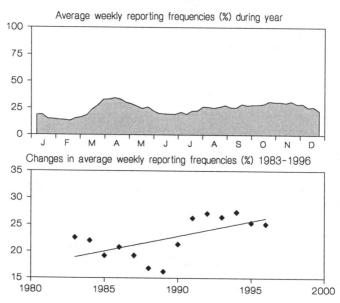

Glaucous Gull
Larus hyperboreus

Annual probability (%) of sighting this species in Wisconsin

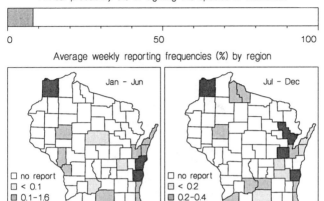

Average weekly reporting frequencies (%) by region

Jan – Jun

☐ no report
☐ < 0.1
▨ 0.1–1.6
■ > 1.6

Jul – Dec

☐ no report
☐ < 0.2
▨ 0.2–0.4
■ > 0.4

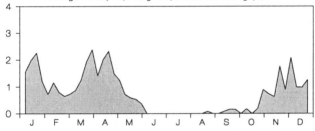

Average weekly reporting frequencies (%) during year

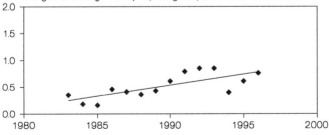

Changes in average weekly reporting frequencies (%) 1983-1996

Caspian Tern
Sterna caspia

Annual probability (%) of sighting this species in Wisconsin

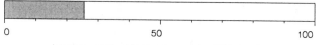

Average weekly reporting frequencies (%) by region

All Months

□ no report
□ < 0.2
▨ 0.2-3.0
■ > 3.0

Average weekly reporting frequencies (%) during year

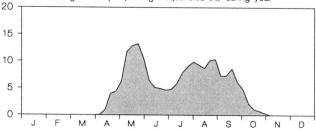

Changes in average weekly reporting frequencies (%) 1983-1996

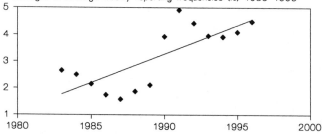

Common Tern
Sterna hirundo

Annual probability (%) of sighting this species in Wisconsin

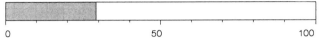

0   50   100

Average weekly reporting frequencies (%) by region

All Months

□ no report
□ < 0.5
▨ 0.5–4.1
■ > 4.1

Average weekly reporting frequencies (%) during year

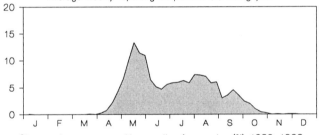

Changes in average weekly reporting frequencies (%) 1983–1996

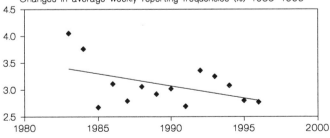

Forster's Tern
Sterna forsteri

Annual probability (%) of sighting this species in Wisconsin

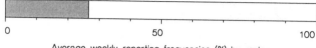

Average weekly reporting frequencies (%) by region

All Months

□ no report
▨ < 0.3
▧ 0.3-3.8
■ > 3.8

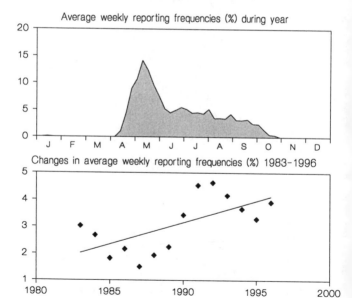

Average weekly reporting frequencies (%) during year

Changes in average weekly reporting frequencies (%) 1983-1996

Black Tern
Chlidonius niger

Annual probability (%) of sighting this species in Wisconsin

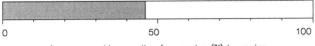

Average weekly reporting frequencies (%) by region

All Months

no report
< 1.1
1.1-8.5
> 8.5

Average weekly reporting frequencies (%) during year

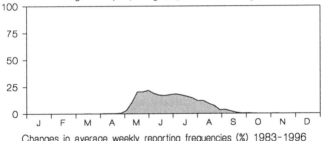

Changes in average weekly reporting frequencies (%) 1983-1996

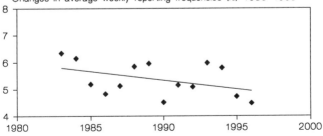

Rock Dove
Columba livia

Annual probability (%) of sighting this species in Wisconsin

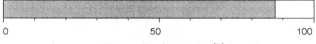

| 0 | 50 | 100 |

Average weekly reporting frequencies (%) by region

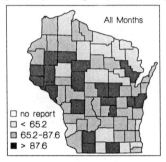

All Months

□ no report
□ < 65.2
▨ 65.2–87.6
■ > 87.6

Average weekly reporting frequencies (%) during year

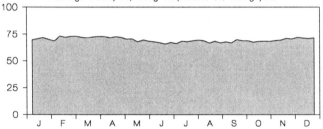

Changes in average weekly reporting frequencies (%) 1983–1996

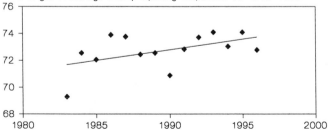

Mourning Dove
Zenaida macroura

Annual probability (%) of sighting this species in Wisconsin

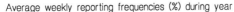

0	50	100

Average weekly reporting frequencies (%) by region

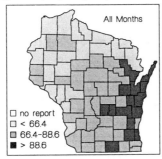

All Months

□ no report
□ < 66.4
▨ 66.4–88.6
■ > 88.6

Average weekly reporting frequencies (%) during year

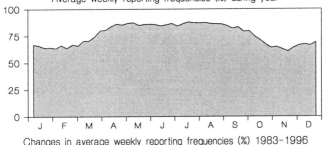

Changes in average weekly reporting frequencies (%) 1983–1996

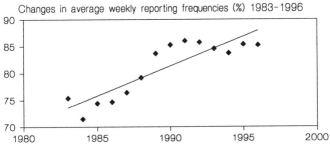

Black-billed Cuckoo
Coccyzus erythropthalmus

Annual probability (%) of sighting this species in Wisconsin

0	50	100

Average weekly reporting frequencies (%) by region

All Months

□ no report
□ < 1.7
▨ 1.7–6.1
■ > 6.1

Average weekly reporting frequencies (%) during year

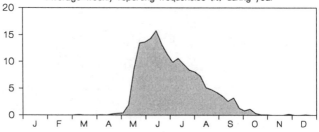

Changes in average weekly reporting frequencies (%) 1983–1996

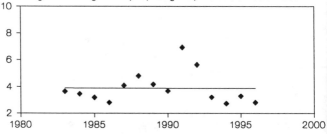

Yellow-billed Cuckoo
Coccyzus americanus

Annual probability (%) of sighting this species in Wisconsin

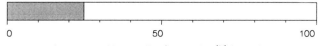

| 0 | 50 | 100 |

Average weekly reporting frequencies (%) by region

All Months

- ☐ no report
- ☐ < 0.5
- ▨ 0.5-2.4
- ■ > 2.4

Average weekly reporting frequencies (%) during year

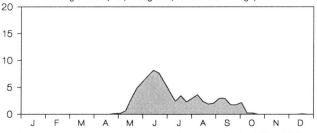

Changes in average weekly reporting frequencies (%) 1983-1996

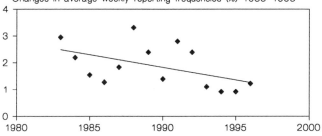

Common Barn-owl
Tyto alba

Annual probability (%) of sighting this species in Wisconsin

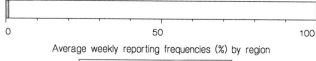

Average weekly reporting frequencies (%) by region

Average weekly reporting frequencies (%) during year

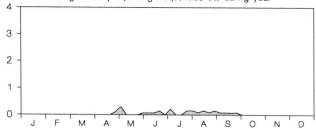

Changes in average weekly reporting frequencies (%) 1983–1996

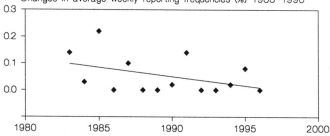

Eastern Screech-owl
Otus asio

Annual probability (%) of sighting this species in Wisconsin

0	50	100

Average weekly reporting frequencies (%) by region

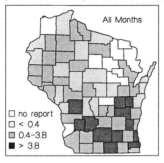

All Months

☐ no report
☐ < 0.4
▨ 0.4-3.8
■ > 3.8

Average weekly reporting frequencies (%) during year

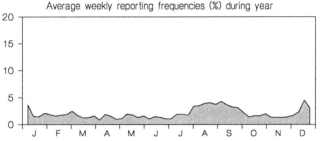

Changes in average weekly reporting frequencies (%) 1983-1996

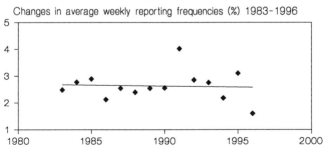

Great Horned Owl
Bubo virginianus

Annual probability (%) of sighting this species in Wisconsin

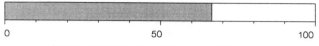

0   50   100

Average weekly reporting frequencies (%) by region

All Months

□ no report
□ < 6.1
▨ 6.1–17.4
■ > 17.4

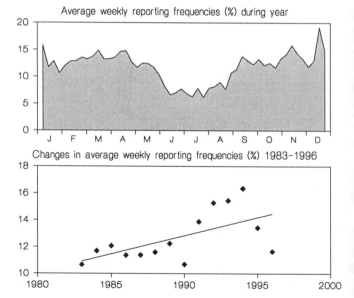

Average weekly reporting frequencies (%) during year

Changes in average weekly reporting frequencies (%) 1983–1996

Snowy Owl
Nyctea scandiaca

Annual probability (%) of sighting this species in Wisconsin

0   50   100

Average weekly reporting frequencies (%) by region

All Months

- □ no report
- □ < 0.2
- ▨ 0.2–1.5
- ■ > 1.5

Average weekly reporting frequencies (%) during year

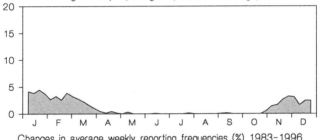

Changes in average weekly reporting frequencies (%) 1983–1996

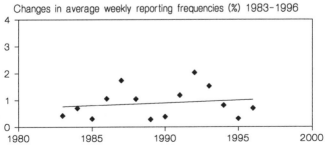

Barred Owl
Strix varia

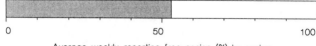

Annual probability (%) of sighting this species in Wisconsin

0	50	100

Average weekly reporting frequencies (%) by region

All Months

☐ no report
☐ < 3.4
▨ 3.4–18.8
■ > 18.8

Average weekly reporting frequencies (%) during year

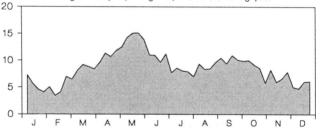

Changes in average weekly reporting frequencies (%) 1983–1996

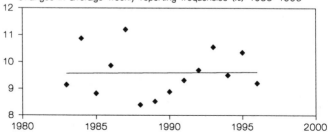

Great Grey Owl
Strix nebulosa

Annual probability (%) of sighting this species in Wisconsin

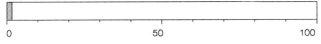

Average weekly reporting frequencies (%) by region

Average weekly reporting frequencies (%) during year

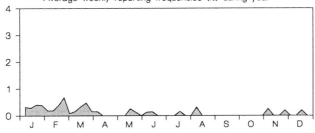

Changes in average weekly reporting frequencies (%) 1983-1996

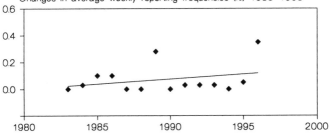

145

Long-eared Owl
Asio otus

Annual probability (%) of sighting this species in Wisconsin

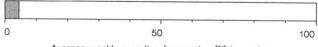

Average weekly reporting frequencies (%) by region

Average weekly reporting frequencies (%) during year

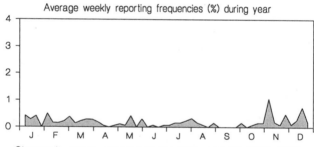

Changes in average weekly reporting frequencies (%) 1983-1996

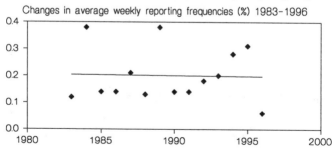

146

Short-eared Owl
Asio flammeus

Annual probability (%) of sighting this species in Wisconsin

Average weekly reporting frequencies (%) by region

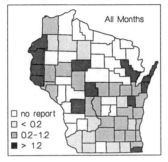

All Months

- □ no report
- □ < 0.2
- ▨ 0.2–1.2
- ■ > 1.2

Average weekly reporting frequencies (%) during year

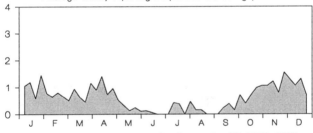

Changes in average weekly reporting frequencies (%) 1983–1996

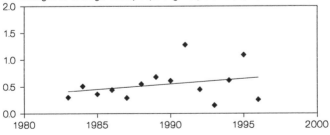

147

Northern Saw-whet Owl
Aegolius acadicus

Annual probability (%) of sighting this species in Wisconsin

0   50   100

Average weekly reporting frequencies (%) by region

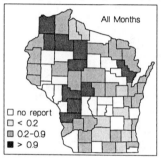

All Months

☐ no report
☐ < 0.2
▨ 0.2-0.9
■ > 0.9

Average weekly reporting frequencies (%) during year

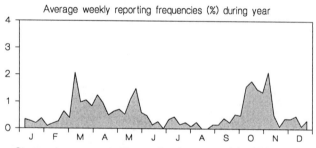

J F M A M J J A S O N D

Changes in average weekly reporting frequencies (%) 1983-1996

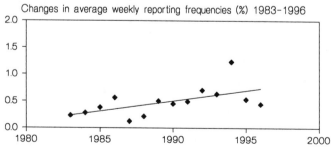

Common Nighthawk
Chordeiles minor

Annual probability (%) of sighting this species in Wisconsin

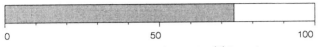

0   50   100

Average weekly reporting frequencies (%) by region

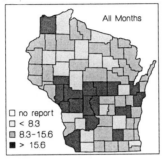

All Months

☐ no report
☐ < 8.3
▨ 8.3–15.6
■ > 15.6

Average weekly reporting frequencies (%) during year

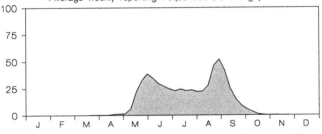

Changes in average weekly reporting frequencies (%) 1983–1996

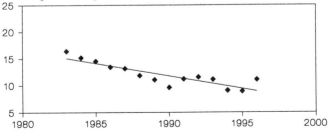

149

Whip-poor-will
Caprimulgus vociferus

Annual probability (%) of sighting this species in Wisconsin

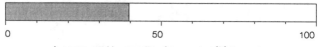

Average weekly reporting frequencies (%) by region

All Months

- □ no report
- ▨ < 0.9
- ▦ 0.9–8.1
- ■ > 8.1

Average weekly reporting frequencies (%) during year

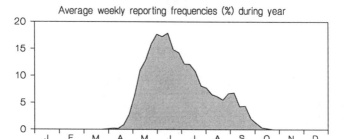

Changes in average weekly reporting frequencies (%) 1983–1996

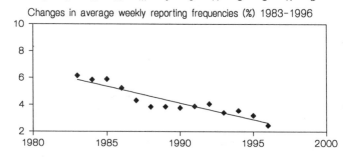

Chimney Swift
Chaetura pelagica

Annual probability (%) of sighting this species in Wisconsin

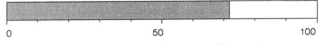

0   50   100

Average weekly reporting frequencies (%) by region

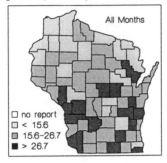

All Months

- □ no report
- □ < 15.6
- ▨ 15.6–26.7
- ■ > 26.7

Average weekly reporting frequencies (%) during year

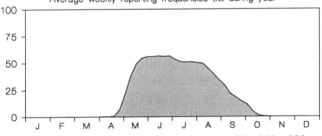

Changes in average weekly reporting frequencies (%) 1983–1996

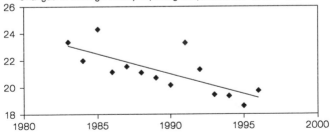

Ruby-throated Hummingbird
Archilochus colubris

Annual probability (%) of sighting this species in Wisconsin

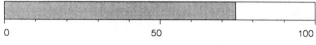

Average weekly reporting frequencies (%) by region

All Months

☐ no report
☐ < 8.5
▨ 8.5-23.6
■ > 23.6

Average weekly reporting frequencies (%) during year

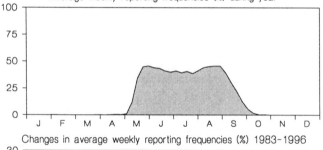

Changes in average weekly reporting frequencies (%) 1983-1996

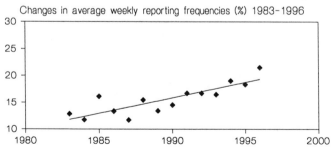

Belted Kingfisher
Ceryle alcyon

Annual probability (%) of sighting this species in Wisconsin

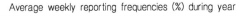

| 0 | 50 | 100 |

Average weekly reporting frequencies (%) by region

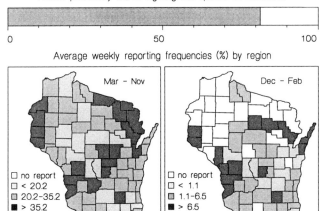

Mar – Nov

Dec – Feb

□ no report
□ < 20.2
▨ 20.2-35.2
■ > 35.2

□ no report
□ < 1.1
▨ 1.1-6.5
■ > 6.5

Average weekly reporting frequencies (%) during year

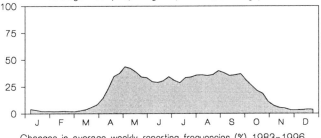

Changes in average weekly reporting frequencies (%) 1983-1996

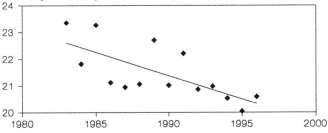

Red-headed Woodpecker
Melanerpes erythrocephalus

Annual probability (%) of sighting this species in Wisconsin

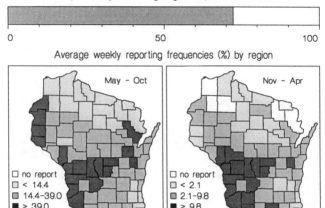

Average weekly reporting frequencies (%) by region

Average weekly reporting frequencies (%) during year

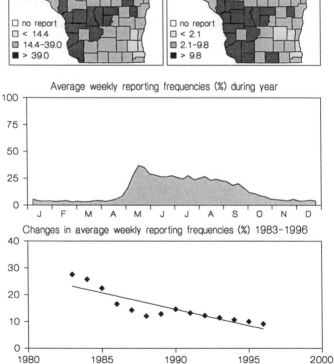

Changes in average weekly reporting frequencies (%) 1983-1996

Red-bellied Woodpecker
Melanerpes carolinus

Annual probability (%) of sighting this species in Wisconsin

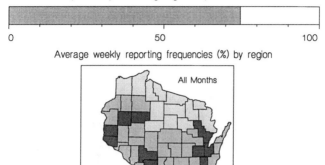

| 0 | 50 | 100 |

Average weekly reporting frequencies (%) by region

All Months

☐ no report
☐ < 9.8
▦ 9.8-39.8
■ > 39.8

Average weekly reporting frequencies (%) during year

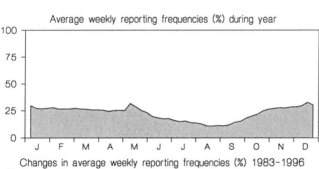

Changes in average weekly reporting frequencies (%) 1983-1996

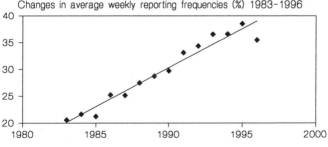

Yellow-bellied Sapsucker
Sphyrapicus varius

Annual probability (%) of sighting this species in Wisconsin

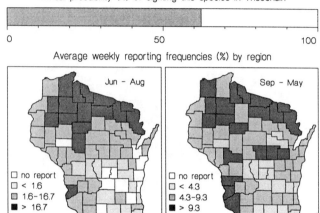

Average weekly reporting frequencies (%) by region

Jun – Aug

☐ no report
☐ < 1.6
▨ 1.6-16.7
■ > 16.7

Sep – May

☐ no report
☐ < 4.3
▨ 4.3-9.3
■ > 9.3

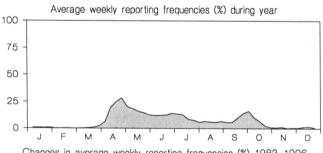

Average weekly reporting frequencies (%) during year

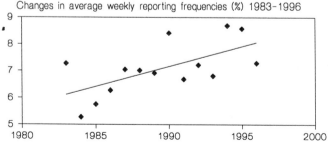

Changes in average weekly reporting frequencies (%) 1983-1996

Downy Woodpecker
Picoides pubescens

Annual probability (%) of sighting this species in Wisconsin

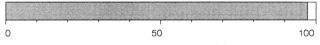

0   50   100

Average weekly reporting frequencies (%) by region

All Months

□ no report
□ < 52.1
▨ 52.1–72.9
■ > 72.9

Average weekly reporting frequencies (%) during year

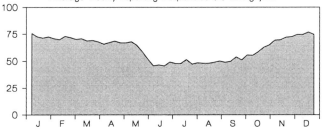

Changes in average weekly reporting frequencies (%) 1983–1996

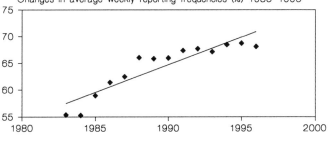

Hairy Woodpecker
Picoides villosus

Annual probability (%) of sighting this species in Wisconsin

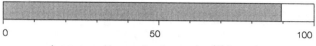

0   50   100

Average weekly reporting frequencies (%) by region

All Months

□ no report
□ < 32.0
▨ 32.0–56.9
■ > 56.9

Average weekly reporting frequencies (%) during year

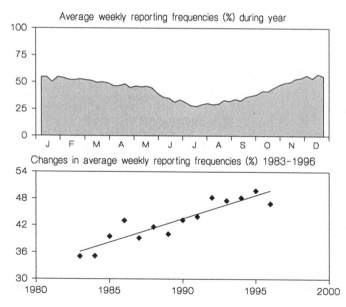

Changes in average weekly reporting frequencies (%) 1983–1996

Northern Flicker
Colaptes auratus

Annual probability (%) of sighting this species in Wisconsin

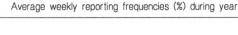

0　　　　　　　　　　　　50　　　　　　　　　　　100

Average weekly reporting frequencies (%) by region

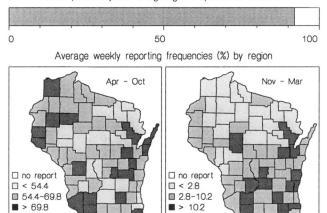

Apr – Oct

☐ no report
☐ < 54.4
▨ 54.4–69.8
■ > 69.8

Nov – Mar

☐ no report
☐ < 2.8
▨ 2.8–10.2
■ > 10.2

Average weekly reporting frequencies (%) during year

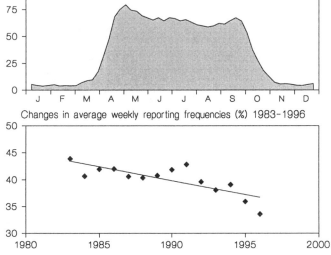

Changes in average weekly reporting frequencies (%) 1983–1996

159

Pileated Woodpecker
Dryocopus pileatus

Annual probability (%) of sighting this species in Wisconsin

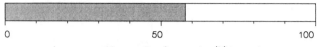

Average weekly reporting frequencies (%) by region

All Months

□ no report
□ < 2.4
▨ 2.4-25.2
■ > 25.2

Average weekly reporting frequencies (%) during year

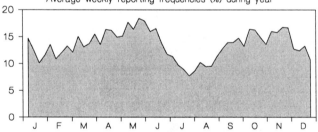

Changes in average weekly reporting frequencies (%) 1983-1996

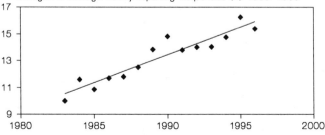

Olive-sided Flycatcher
Contopus borealis

Annual probability (%) of sighting this species in Wisconsin

0　　　　　　　　　　　　　50　　　　　　　　　　　　100

Average weekly reporting frequencies (%) by region

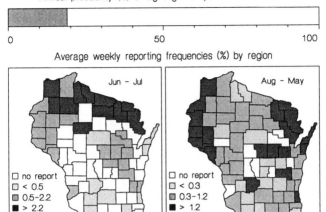

Jun – Jul

☐ no report
☐ < 0.5
▨ 0.5-2.2
■ > 2.2

Aug – May

☐ no report
☐ < 0.3
▨ 0.3-1.2
■ > 1.2

Average weekly reporting frequencies (%) during year

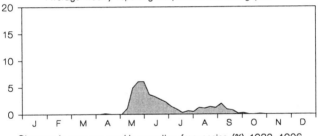

Changes in average weekly reporting frequencies (%) 1983-1996

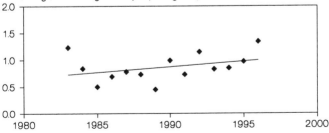

161

Eastern Wood-pewee
Contopus virens

Annual probability (%) of sighting this species in Wisconsin

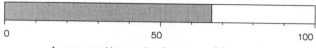

Average weekly reporting frequencies (%) by region

Average weekly reporting frequencies (%) during year

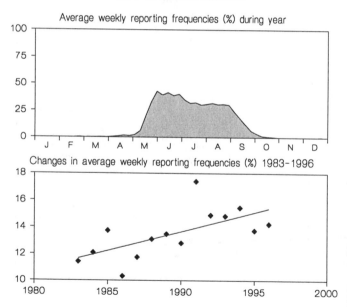

Changes in average weekly reporting frequencies (%) 1983-1996

Yellow-bellied Flycatcher
Empidonax flaviventris

Annual probability (%) of sighting this species in Wisconsin

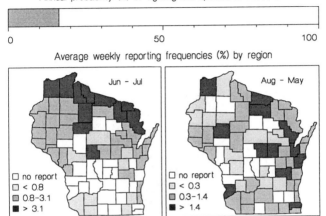

Average weekly reporting frequencies (%) by region

Jun – Jul

Aug – May

☐ no report
☐ < 0.8
▨ 0.8–3.1
■ > 3.1

☐ no report
☐ < 0.3
▨ 0.3–1.4
■ > 1.4

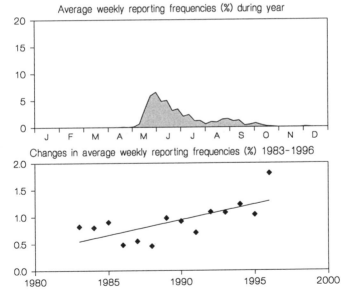

Average weekly reporting frequencies (%) during year

Changes in average weekly reporting frequencies (%) 1983–1996

Acadian Flycatcher
Empidonax virescens

Annual probability (%) of sighting this species in Wisconsin

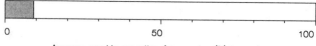

Average weekly reporting frequencies (%) by region

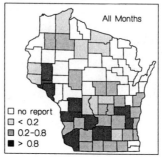

All Months

□ no report
□ < 0.2
▨ 0.2-0.8
■ > 0.8

Average weekly reporting frequencies (%) during year

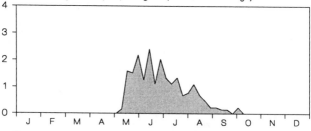

Changes in average weekly reporting frequencies (%) 1983-1996

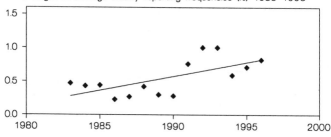

Alder Flycatcher
Empidonax alnorum

Annual probability (%) of sighting this species in Wisconsin

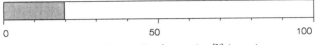

0   50   100

Average weekly reporting frequencies (%) by region

All Months

☐ no report
☐ < 0.4
▨ 0.4-2.6
■ > 2.6

Average weekly reporting frequencies (%) during year

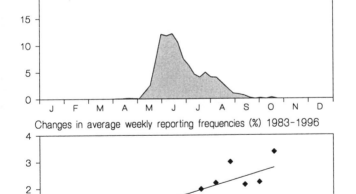

Changes in average weekly reporting frequencies (%) 1983-1996

Willow Flycatcher
Empidonax traillii

Annual probability (%) of sighting this species in Wisconsin

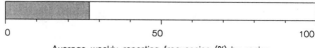

0   50   100

Average weekly reporting frequencies (%) by region

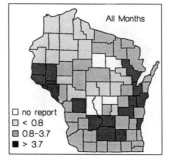

All Months

☐ no report
☐ < 0.8
▨ 0.8–3.7
■ > 3.7

Average weekly reporting frequencies (%) during year

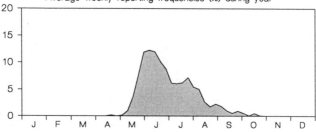

Changes in average weekly reporting frequencies (%) 1983–1996

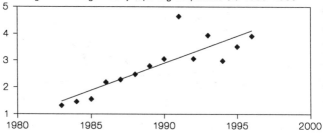

Least Flycatcher
Empidonax minimus

Annual probability (%) of sighting this species in Wisconsin

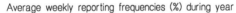

0   50   100

Average weekly reporting frequencies (%) by region

All Months

no report
< 3.0
3.0-8.4
> 8.4

Average weekly reporting frequencies (%) during year

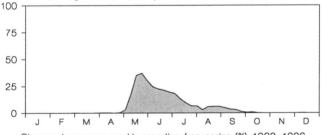

Changes in average weekly reporting frequencies (%) 1983-1996

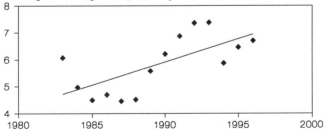

Eastern Phoebe
Sayornis phoebe

Annual probability (%) of sighting this species in Wisconsin

| 0 | 50 | 100 |

Average weekly reporting frequencies (%) by region

All Months

□ no report
□ < 9.9
▨ 9.9–25.5
■ > 25.5

Average weekly reporting frequencies (%) during year

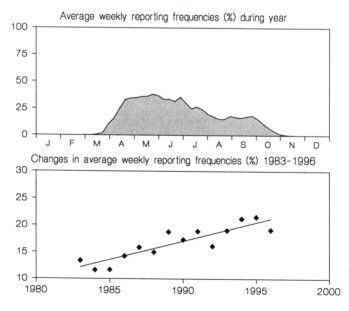

Changes in average weekly reporting frequencies (%) 1983–1996

Great Crested Flycatcher
Myiarchus crinitus

Annual probability (%) of sighting this species in Wisconsin

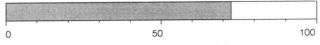

0   50   100

Average weekly reporting frequencies (%) by region

All Months

☐ no report
☐ < 9.5
▨ 9.5–17.4
■ > 17.4

Average weekly reporting frequencies (%) during year

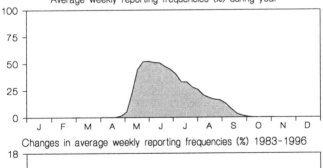

Changes in average weekly reporting frequencies (%) 1983–1996

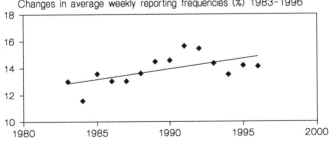

Eastern Kingbird
Tyrannus tyrannus

Annual probability (%) of sighting this species in Wisconsin

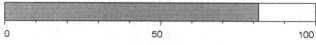

0	50	100

Average weekly reporting frequencies (%) by region

All Months

□ no report
□ < 17.8
▨ 17.8-27.9
■ > 27.9

Average weekly reporting frequencies (%) during year

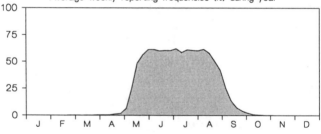

Changes in average weekly reporting frequencies (%) 1983-1996

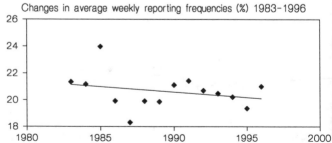

Horned Lark
Eremophila alpestris

Annual probability (%) of sighting this species in Wisconsin

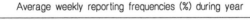

0	50	100

Average weekly reporting frequencies (%) by region

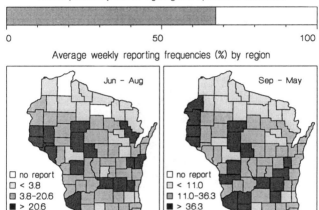

Jun – Aug

☐ no report
☐ < 3.8
▨ 3.8-20.6
■ > 20.6

Sep – May

☐ no report
☐ < 11.0
▨ 11.0-36.3
■ > 36.3

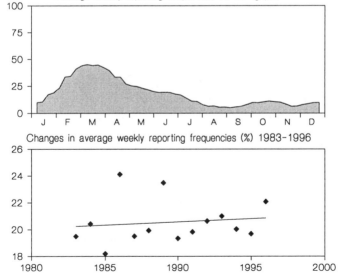

Average weekly reporting frequencies (%) during year

Changes in average weekly reporting frequencies (%) 1983-1996

Purple Martin
Progne subis

Annual probability (%) of sighting this species in Wisconsin

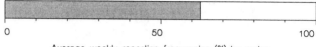

Average weekly reporting frequencies (%) by region

Average weekly reporting frequencies (%) during year

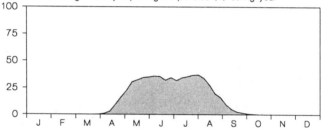

Changes in average weekly reporting frequencies (%) 1983-1996

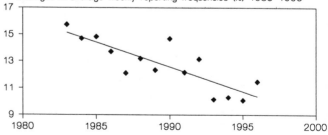

Tree Swallow
Tachycineta bicolor

Annual probability (%) of sighting this species in Wisconsin

0	50	100

Average weekly reporting frequencies (%) by region

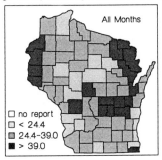

All Months

□ no report
□ < 24.4
▨ 24.4-39.0
■ > 39.0

Average weekly reporting frequencies (%) during year

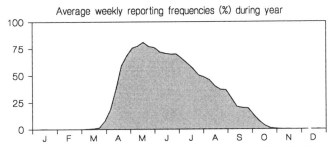

Changes in average weekly reporting frequencies (%) 1983-1996

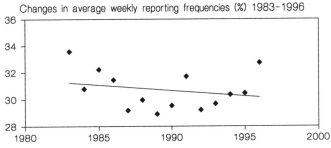

Northern Rough-winged Swallow
Stelgidopteryx serripennis

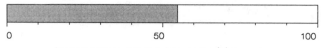

Annual probability (%) of sighting this species in Wisconsin

0   50   100

Average weekly reporting frequencies (%) by region

All Months

☐ no report
☐ < 3.8
▨ 3.8–9.5
■ > 9.5

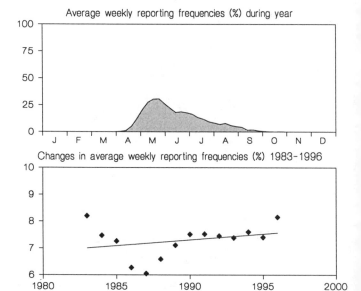

Average weekly reporting frequencies (%) during year

J F M A M J J A S O N D

Changes in average weekly reporting frequencies (%) 1983–1996

Bank Swallow
Riparia riparia

Annual probability (%) of sighting this species in Wisconsin

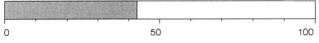

0　　　　　　　　　50　　　　　　　　　100

Average weekly reporting frequencies (%) by region

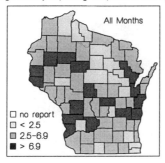

All Months

☐ no report
☐ < 2.5
▨ 2.5-6.9
■ > 6.9

Average weekly reporting frequencies (%) during year

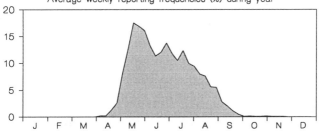

Changes in average weekly reporting frequencies (%) 1983-1996

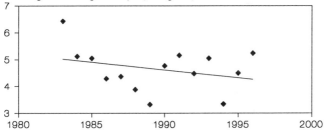

Cliff Swallow
Hirundo pyrrhonota

Annual probability (%) of sighting this species in Wisconsin

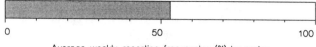

Average weekly reporting frequencies (%) by region

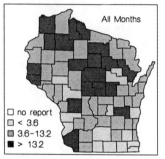

All Months

□ no report
☐ < 3.6
▨ 3.6-13.2
■ > 13.2

Average weekly reporting frequencies (%) during year

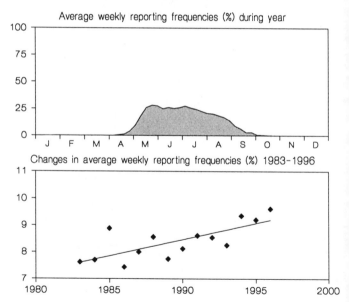

Changes in average weekly reporting frequencies (%) 1983-1996

Barn Swallow
Hirundo rustica

Annual probability (%) of sighting this species in Wisconsin

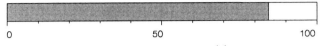

| 0 | 50 | 100 |

Average weekly reporting frequencies (%) by region

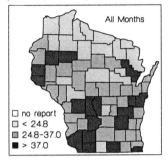

All Months

- ☐ no report
- < 24.8
- 24.8–37.0
- > 37.0

Average weekly reporting frequencies (%) during year

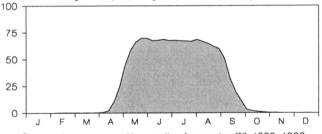

Changes in average weekly reporting frequencies (%) 1983–1996

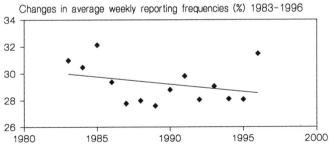

Gray Jay
Perisoreus canadensis

Annual probability (%) of sighting this species in Wisconsin

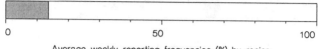

| 0 | 50 | 100 |

Average weekly reporting frequencies (%) by region

All Months

☐ no report
☐ < 0.1
▨ 0.1–2.1
■ > 2.1

Average weekly reporting frequencies (%) during year

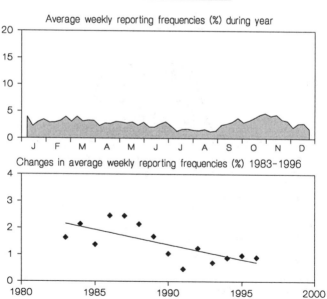

Changes in average weekly reporting frequencies (%) 1983–1996

Blue Jay
Cyanocitta cristata

Annual probability (%) of sighting this species in Wisconsin

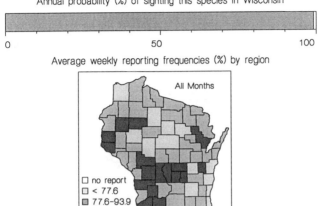

0   50   100

Average weekly reporting frequencies (%) by region

All Months

□ no report
□ < 77.6
▨ 77.6–93.9
■ > 93.9

Average weekly reporting frequencies (%) during year

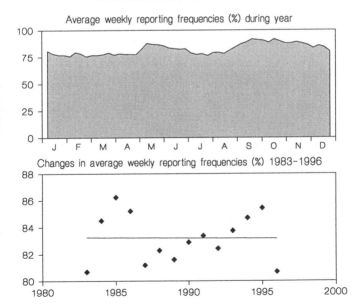

Changes in average weekly reporting frequencies (%) 1983–1996

179

American Crow
Corvus brachyrhynchos

Annual probability (%) of sighting this species in Wisconsin

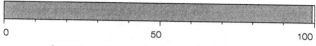

| 0 | 50 | 100 |

Average weekly reporting frequencies (%) by region

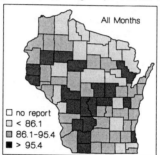

All Months

- □ no report
- □ < 86.1
- ▨ 86.1-95.4
- ■ > 95.4

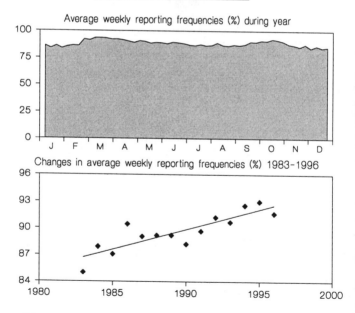

Average weekly reporting frequencies (%) during year

Changes in average weekly reporting frequencies (%) 1983-1996

Common Raven
Corvus corax

Annual probability (%) of sighting this species in Wisconsin

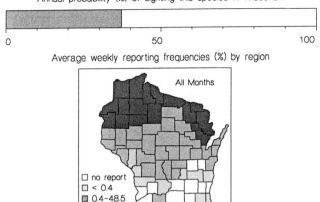

Average weekly reporting frequencies (%) by region

All Months

- □ no report
- □ < 0.4
- ▨ 0.4–48.5
- ■ > 48.5

Average weekly reporting frequencies (%) during year

Changes in average weekly reporting frequencies (%) 1983–1996

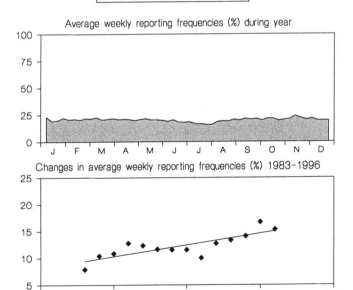

Black-capped Chickadee
Parus atricapillus

Annual probability (%) of sighting this species in Wisconsin

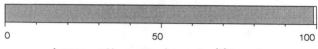

0	50	100

Average weekly reporting frequencies (%) by region

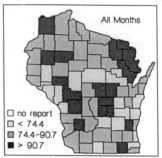

All Months

- □ no report
- ▨ < 74.4
- ▨ 74.4–90.7
- ■ > 90.7

Average weekly reporting frequencies (%) during year

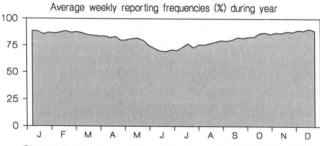

Changes in average weekly reporting frequencies (%) 1983–1996

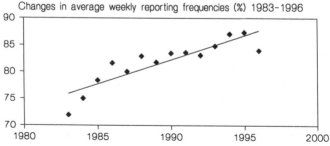

Boreal Chickadee
Parus hudsonicus

Annual probability (%) of sighting this species in Wisconsin

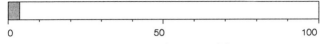

0   50   100

Average weekly reporting frequencies (%) by region

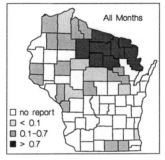

All Months

□ no report
□ < 0.1
▨ 0.1–0.7
■ > 0.7

Average weekly reporting frequencies (%) during year

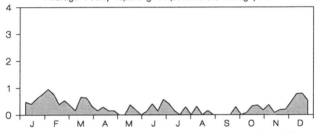

Changes in average weekly reporting frequencies (%) 1983–1996

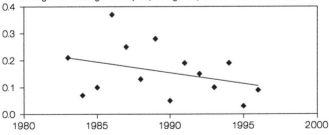

Tufted Titmouse
Parus bicolor

Annual probability (%) of sighting this species in Wisconsin

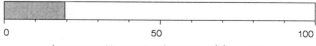

0   50   100

Average weekly reporting frequencies (%) by region

Average weekly reporting frequencies (%) during year

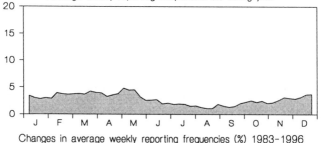

Red-breasted Nuthatch
Sitta canadensis

Annual probability (%) of sighting this species in Wisconsin

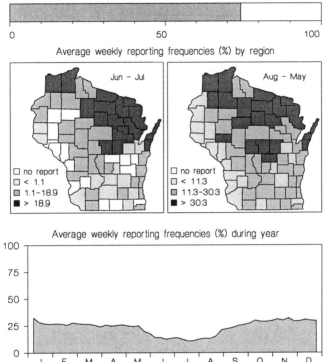

Average weekly reporting frequencies (%) by region

Jun – Jul

Aug – May

□ no report
□ < 1.1
▨ 1.1–18.9
■ > 18.9

□ no report
□ < 11.3
▨ 11.3–30.3
■ > 30.3

Average weekly reporting frequencies (%) during year

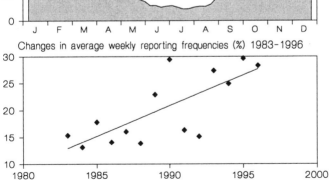

Changes in average weekly reporting frequencies (%) 1983–1996

White-breasted Nuthatch
Sitta carolinensis

Annual probability (%) of sighting this species in Wisconsin

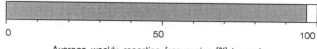

0   50   100

Average weekly reporting frequencies (%) by region

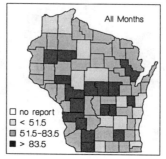

All Months

- □ no report
- □ < 51.5
- ▨ 51.5–83.5
- ■ > 83.5

Average weekly reporting frequencies (%) during year

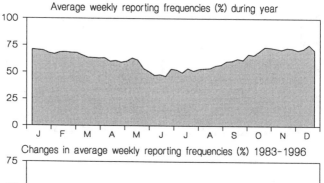

Changes in average weekly reporting frequencies (%) 1983–1996

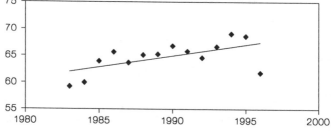

Brown Creeper
Certhia americana

Annual probability (%) of sighting this species in Wisconsin

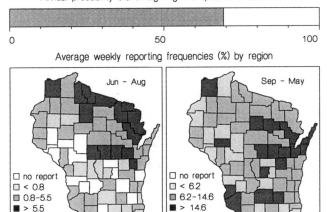

Average weekly reporting frequencies (%) by region

Jun – Aug

Sep – May

□ no report
□ < 0.8
▦ 0.8-5.5
■ > 5.5

□ no report
□ < 6.2
▦ 6.2-14.6
■ > 14.6

Average weekly reporting frequencies (%) during year

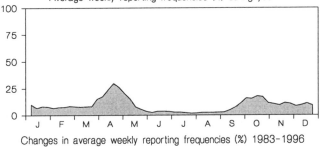

Changes in average weekly reporting frequencies (%) 1983-1996

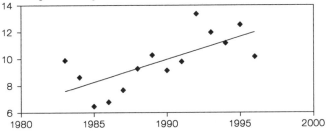

House Wren
Troglodytes aedon

Annual probability (%) of sighting this species in Wisconsin

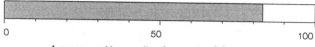

0   50   100

Average weekly reporting frequencies (%) by region

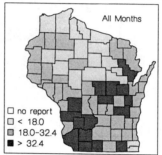

All Months

☐ no report
☐ < 18.0
▨ 18.0-32.4
■ > 32.4

Average weekly reporting frequencies (%) during year

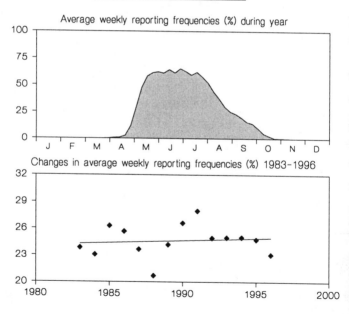

Changes in average weekly reporting frequencies (%) 1983-1996

Winter Wren
Troglodytes troglodytes

Annual probability (%) of sighting this species in Wisconsin

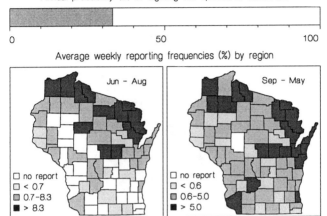

Average weekly reporting frequencies (%) by region

Jun – Aug

Sep – May

□ no report
□ < 0.7
▨ 0.7–8.3
■ > 8.3

□ no report
□ < 0.6
▨ 0.6–5.0
■ > 5.0

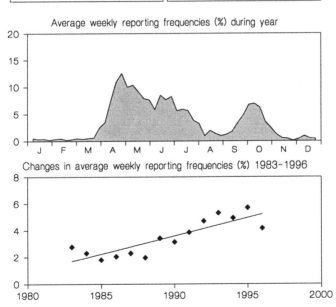

Average weekly reporting frequencies (%) during year

Changes in average weekly reporting frequencies (%) 1983–1996

Sedge Wren
Cistothorus platensis

Annual probability (%) of sighting this species in Wisconsin

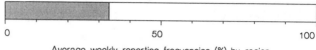

| 0 | 50 | 100 |

Average weekly reporting frequencies (%) by region

All Months

☐ no report
☐ < 1.5
▨ 1.5–5.9
■ > 5.9

Average weekly reporting frequencies (%) during year

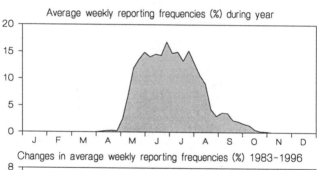

Changes in average weekly reporting frequencies (%) 1983–1996

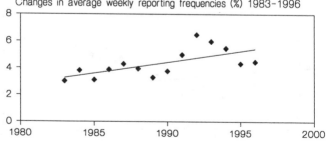

Marsh Wren
Cistothorus palustris

Annual probability (%) of sighting this species in Wisconsin

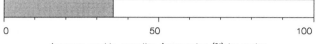

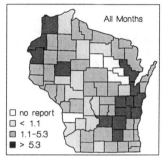

Average weekly reporting frequencies (%) by region

All Months

□ no report
□ < 1.1
▨ 1.1-5.3
■ > 5.3

Average weekly reporting frequencies (%) during year

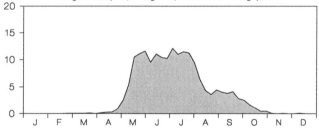

Changes in average weekly reporting frequencies (%) 1983-1996

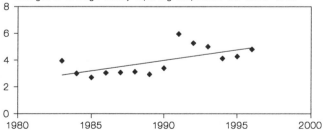

Golden-crowned Kinglet
Regulus satrapa

Annual probability (%) of sighting this species in Wisconsin

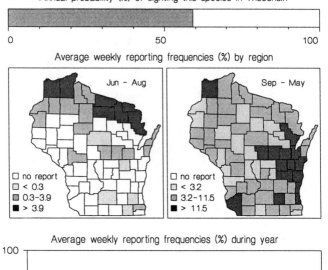

Average weekly reporting frequencies (%) by region

Average weekly reporting frequencies (%) during year

Changes in average weekly reporting frequencies (%) 1983-1996

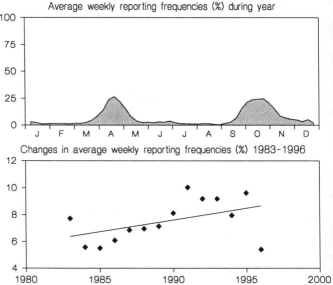

Ruby-crowned Kinglet
Regulus calendula

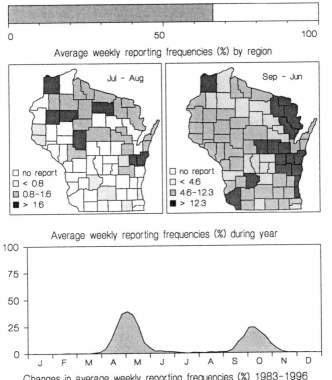

Annual probability (%) of sighting this species in Wisconsin

0   50   100

Average weekly reporting frequencies (%) by region

Jul – Aug

Sep – Jun

□ no report
□ < 0.8
▨ 0.8-1.6
■ > 1.6

□ no report
□ < 4.6
▨ 4.6-12.3
■ > 12.3

Average weekly reporting frequencies (%) during year

J F M A M J J A S O N D

Changes in average weekly reporting frequencies (%) 1983-1996

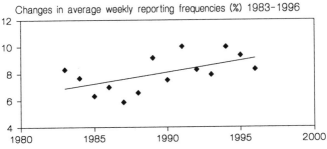

Blue-gray Gnatcatcher
Polioptila caerulea

Annual probability (%) of sighting this species in Wisconsin

| 0 | 50 | 100 |

Average weekly reporting frequencies (%) by region

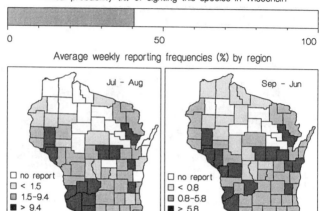

Jul – Aug

- □ no report
- □ < 1.5
- ▨ 1.5–9.4
- ■ > 9.4

Sep – Jun

- □ no report
- □ < 0.8
- ▨ 0.8–5.8
- ■ > 5.8

Average weekly reporting frequencies (%) during year

Changes in average weekly reporting frequencies (%) 1983–1996

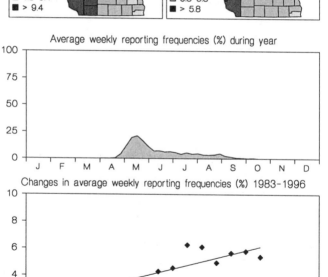

Eastern Bluebird
Sialia sialis

Annual probability (%) of sighting this species in Wisconsin

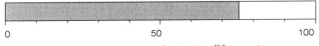

| 0 | 50 | 100 |

Average weekly reporting frequencies (%) by region

All Months

□ no report
□ < 12.8
▨ 12.8–41.1
■ > 41.1

Average weekly reporting frequencies (%) during year

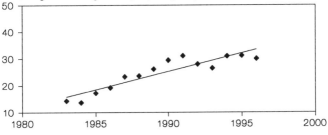

Changes in average weekly reporting frequencies (%) 1983–1996

Veery
Catharus fuscescens

Annual probability (%) of sighting this species in Wisconsin

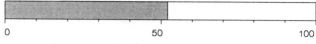

0	50	100

Average weekly reporting frequencies (%) by region

All Months

□ no report
□ < 2.0
▨ 2.0-9.0
■ > 9.0

Average weekly reporting frequencies (%) during year

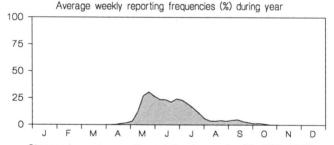

Changes in average weekly reporting frequencies (%) 1983-1996

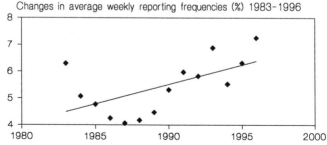

Gray-cheeked Thrush
Catharus minimus

Annual probability (%) of sighting this species in Wisconsin

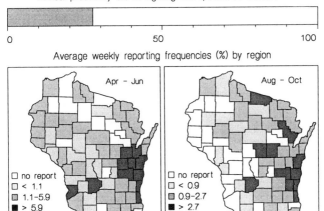

Average weekly reporting frequencies (%) by region

Apr – Jun

Aug – Oct

☐ no report
☐ < 1.1
▨ 1.1–5.9
■ > 5.9

☐ no report
☐ < 0.9
▨ 0.9–2.7
■ > 2.7

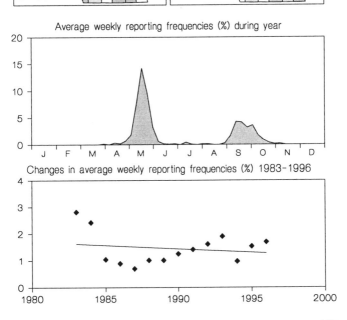

Average weekly reporting frequencies (%) during year

Changes in average weekly reporting frequencies (%) 1983–1996

Swainson's Thrush
Catharus ustulatus

Annual probability (%) of sighting this species in Wisconsin

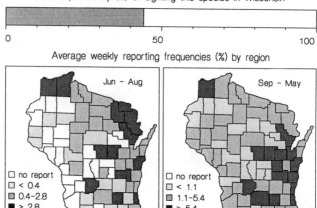

Average weekly reporting frequencies (%) by region

Jun – Aug

☐ no report
☐ < 0.4
▨ 0.4-2.8
■ > 2.8

Sep – May

☐ no report
☐ < 1.1
▨ 1.1-5.4
■ > 5.4

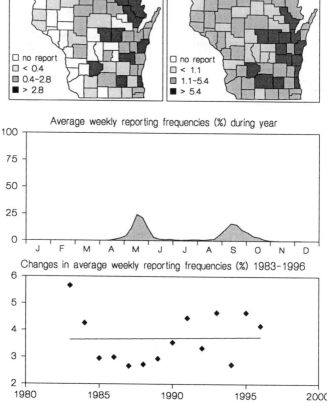

Average weekly reporting frequencies (%) during year

Changes in average weekly reporting frequencies (%) 1983-1996

Hermit Thrush
Catharus guttatus

Annual probability (%) of sighting this species in Wisconsin

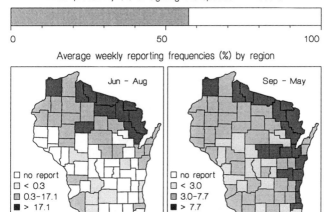

Average weekly reporting frequencies (%) by region

Jun – Aug

Sep – May

□ no report
□ < 0.3
▤ 0.3-17.1
■ > 17.1

□ no report
□ < 3.0
■ 3.0-7.7
■ > 7.7

Average weekly reporting frequencies (%) during year

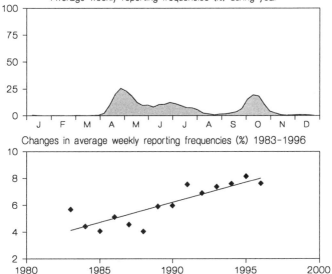

Changes in average weekly reporting frequencies (%) 1983-1996

Wood Thrush
Hylocichla mustelina

Annual probability (%) of sighting this species in Wisconsin

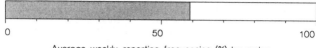

0   50   100

Average weekly reporting frequencies (%) by region

All Months

☐ no report
☐ < 3.8
▨ 3.8–9.9
■ > 9.9

Average weekly reporting frequencies (%) during year

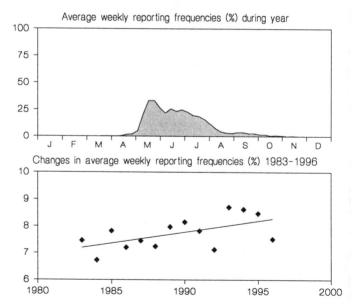

Changes in average weekly reporting frequencies (%) 1983–1996

American Robin
Turdus migratorius

Annual probability (%) of sighting this species in Wisconsin

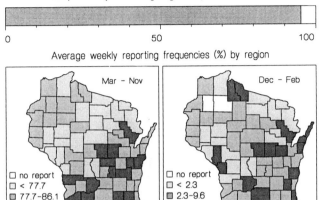

Average weekly reporting frequencies (%) by region

Average weekly reporting frequencies (%) during year

Changes in average weekly reporting frequencies (%) 1983-1996

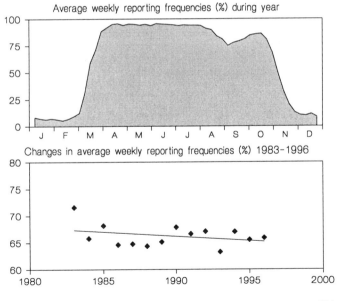

Gray Catbird
Dumetella carolinensis

Annual probability (%) of sighting this species in Wisconsin

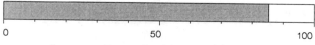

| 0 | 50 | 100 |

Average weekly reporting frequencies (%) by region

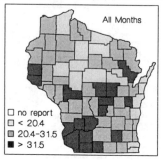

All Months

☐ no report
☐ < 20.4
▨ 20.4-31.5
■ > 31.5

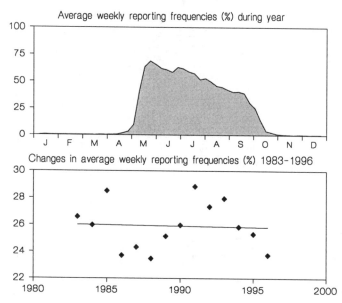

Average weekly reporting frequencies (%) during year

Changes in average weekly reporting frequencies (%) 1983-1996

Northern Mockingbird
Mimus polyglottos

Annual probability (%) of sighting this species in Wisconsin

Average weekly reporting frequencies (%) by region

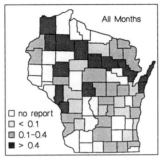

All Months

- □ no report
- □ < 0.1
- ▨ 0.1–0.4
- ■ > 0.4

Average weekly reporting frequencies (%) during year

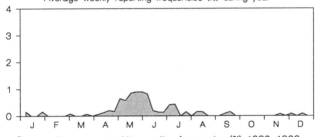

Changes in average weekly reporting frequencies (%) 1983–1996

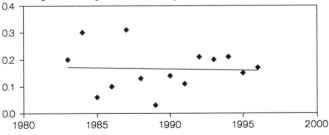

Brown Thrasher
Toxostoma rufum

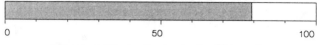

Annual probability (%) of sighting this species in Wisconsin

| 0 | 50 | 100 |

Average weekly reporting frequencies (%) by region

All Months

☐ no report
☐ < 12.0
▨ 12.0–21.7
■ > 21.7

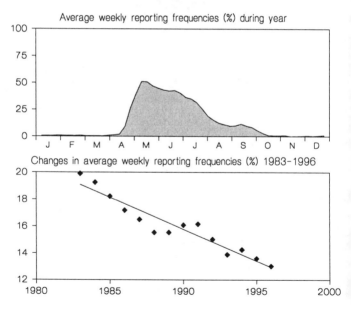

Average weekly reporting frequencies (%) during year

Changes in average weekly reporting frequencies (%) 1983–1996

204

Water Pipit
Anthus spinoletta

Annual probability (%) of sighting this species in Wisconsin

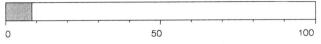

0   50   100

Average weekly reporting frequencies (%) by region

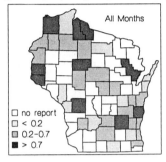

All Months

□ no report
□ < 0.2
▨ 0.2–0.7
■ > 0.7

Average weekly reporting frequencies (%) during year

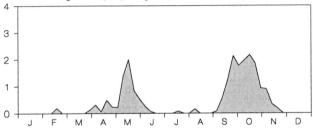

Changes in average weekly reporting frequencies (%) 1983–1996

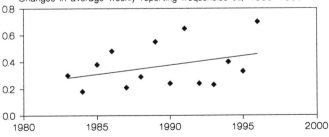

Bohemian Waxwing
Bombycilla garrulus

Annual probability (%) of sighting this species in Wisconsin

0   50   100

Average weekly reporting frequencies (%) by region

All Months

☐ no report
☐ < 0.2
▨ 0.2-1.1
■ > 1.1

Average weekly reporting frequencies (%) during year

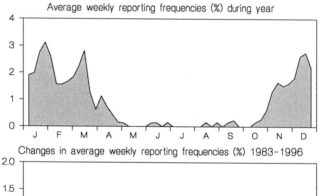

Changes in average weekly reporting frequencies (%) 1983-1996

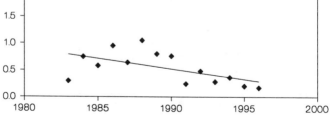

Cedar Waxwing
Bombycilla cedrorum

Annual probability (%) of sighting this species in Wisconsin

0   50   100

Average weekly reporting frequencies (%) by region

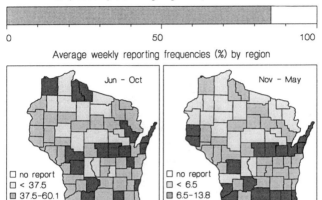

Jun – Oct

- □ no report
- □ < 37.5
- ▨ 37.5–60.1
- ■ > 60.1

Nov – May

- □ no report
- □ < 6.5
- ▨ 6.5–13.8
- ■ > 13.8

Average weekly reporting frequencies (%) during year

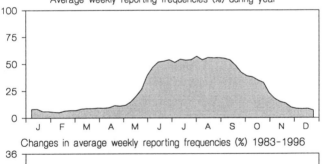

Changes in average weekly reporting frequencies (%) 1983–1996

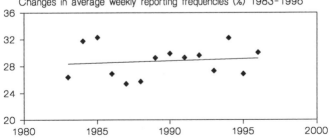

Northern Shrike
Lanius excubitor

Annual probability (%) of sighting this species in Wisconsin

Average weekly reporting frequencies (%) by region

All Months

☐ no report
☐ < 1.1
▨ 1.1–6.7
■ > 6.7

Average weekly reporting frequencies (%) during year

Changes in average weekly reporting frequencies (%) 1983–1996

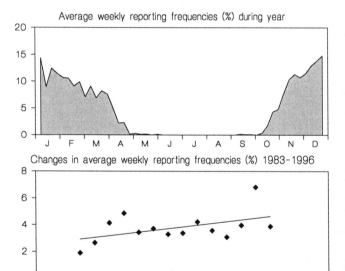

Loggerhead Shrike
Lanius ludovicianus

Annual probability (%) of sighting this species in Wisconsin

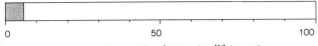

0	50	100

Average weekly reporting frequencies (%) by region

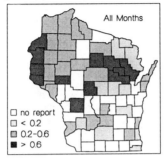

All Months

☐ no report
☐ < 0.2
▨ 0.2-0.6
■ > 0.6

Average weekly reporting frequencies (%) during year

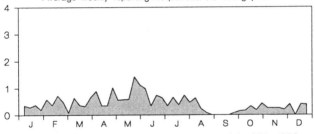

Changes in average weekly reporting frequencies (%) 1983-1996

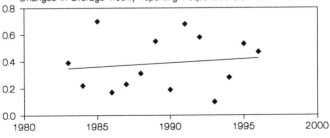

209

European Starling
Sturnus vulgaris

Annual probability (%) of sighting this species in Wisconsin

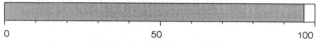

0   50   100

Average weekly reporting frequencies (%) by region

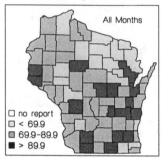

All Months

☐ no report
☐ < 69.9
▨ 69.9–89.9
■ > 89.9

Average weekly reporting frequencies (%) during year

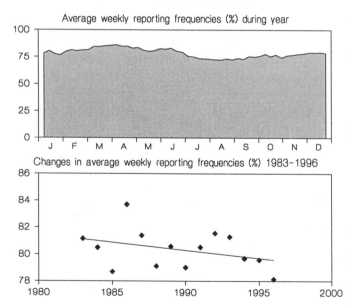

Changes in average weekly reporting frequencies (%) 1983–1996

210

Bell's Vireo
Vireo bellii

Annual probability (%) of sighting this species in Wisconsin

0   50   100

Average weekly reporting frequencies (%) by region

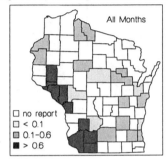

All Months

□ no report
□ < 0.1
▨ 0.1–0.6
■ > 0.6

Average weekly reporting frequencies (%) during year

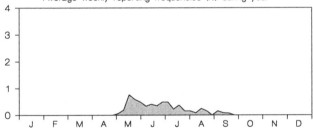

J F M A M J J A S O N D

Changes in average weekly reporting frequencies (%) 1983–1996

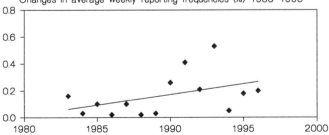

Solitary Vireo
Vireo solitarius

Annual probability (%) of sighting this species in Wisconsin

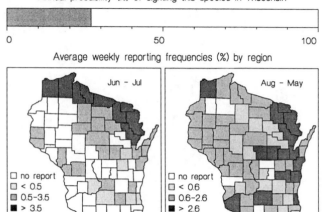

Average weekly reporting frequencies (%) by region

Jun – Jul

Aug – May

☐ no report
☐ < 0.5
▨ 0.5-3.5
■ > 3.5

☐ no report
☐ < 0.6
▨ 0.6-2.6
■ > 2.6

Average weekly reporting frequencies (%) during year

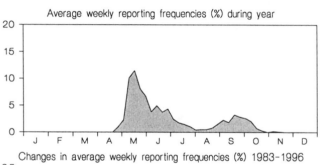

Changes in average weekly reporting frequencies (%) 1983-1996

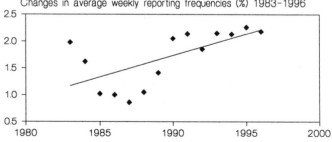

Yellow-throated Vireo
Vireo flavifrons

Annual probability (%) of sighting this species in Wisconsin

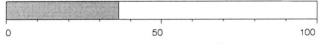

Average weekly reporting frequencies (%) by region

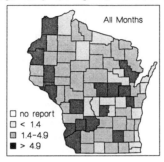

Average weekly reporting frequencies (%) during year

Changes in average weekly reporting frequencies (%) 1983-1996

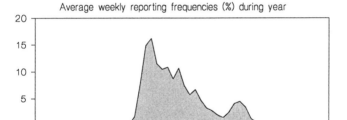

Warbling Vireo
Vireo gilvus

Annual probability (%) of sighting this species in Wisconsin

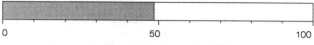

Average weekly reporting frequencies (%) by region

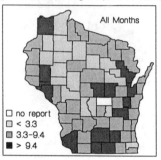

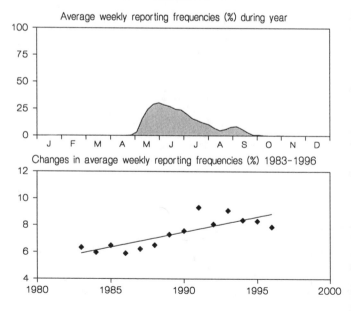

Philadelphia Vireo
Vireo philadelphicus

Annual probability (%) of sighting this species in Wisconsin

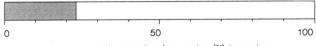

0   50   100

Average weekly reporting frequencies (%) by region

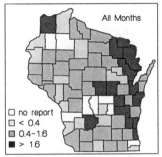

Average weekly reporting frequencies (%) during year

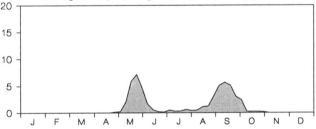

Changes in average weekly reporting frequencies (%) 1983–1996

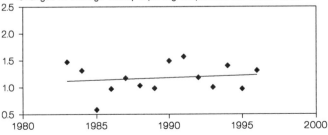

Red-eyed Vireo
Vireo olivaceus

Annual probability (%) of sighting this species in Wisconsin

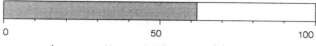

Average weekly reporting frequencies (%) by region

Average weekly reporting frequencies (%) during year

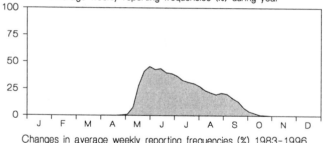

Changes in average weekly reporting frequencies (%) 1983-1996

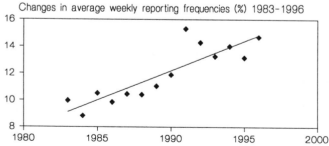

Blue-winged Warbler
Vermivora pinus

Annual probability (%) of sighting this species in Wisconsin

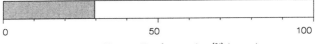

0   50   100

Average weekly reporting frequencies (%) by region

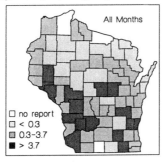

All Months

☐ no report
☐ < 0.3
▨ 0.3-3.7
■ > 3.7

Average weekly reporting frequencies (%) during year

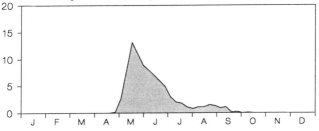

Changes in average weekly reporting frequencies (%) 1983-1996

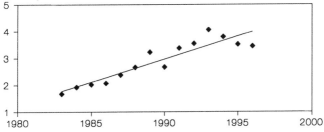

Golden-winged Warbler
Vermivora chrysoptera

Annual probability (%) of sighting this species in Wisconsin

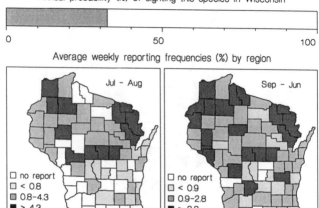

Average weekly reporting frequencies (%) by region

Jul – Aug	Sep – Jun
□ no report	□ no report
□ < 0.8	□ < 0.9
▨ 0.8-4.3	▨ 0.9-2.8
■ > 4.3	■ > 2.8

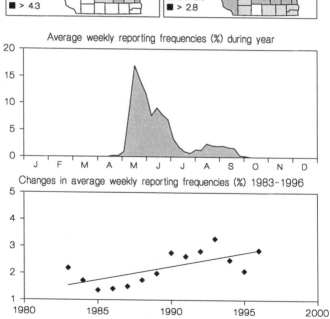

Average weekly reporting frequencies (%) during year

Changes in average weekly reporting frequencies (%) 1983-1996

Tennessee Warbler
Vermivora peregrina

Annual probability (%) of sighting this species in Wisconsin

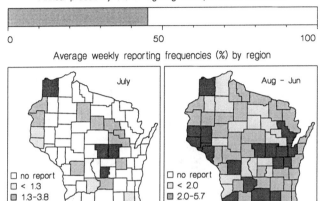

Average weekly reporting frequencies (%) by region

July

Aug – Jun

□ no report
□ < 1.3
▨ 1.3-3.8
■ > 3.8

□ no report
□ < 2.0
▨ 2.0-5.7
■ > 5.7

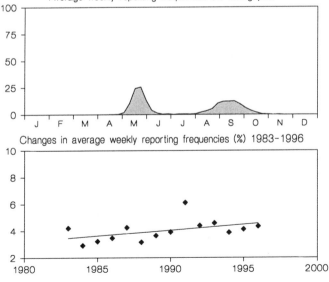

Average weekly reporting frequencies (%) during year

Changes in average weekly reporting frequencies (%) 1983-1996

Orange-crowned Warbler
Vermivora celata

Annual probability (%) of sighting this species in Wisconsin

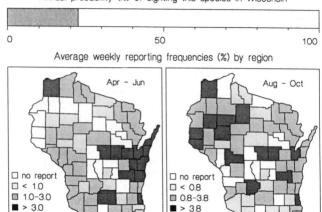

Average weekly reporting frequencies (%) by region

Apr – Jun

Aug – Oct

☐ no report
☐ < 1.0
▨ 1.0–3.0
■ > 3.0

☐ no report
☐ < 0.8
▨ 0.8–3.8
■ > 3.8

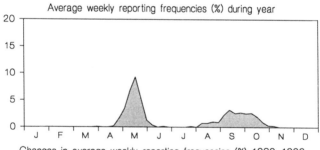

Average weekly reporting frequencies (%) during year

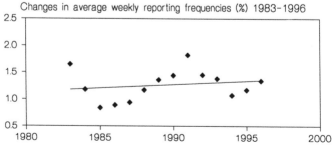

Changes in average weekly reporting frequencies (%) 1983–1996

220

Nashville Warbler
Vermivora ruficapilla

Annual probability (%) of sighting this species in Wisconsin

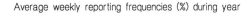

0   50   100

Average weekly reporting frequencies (%) by region

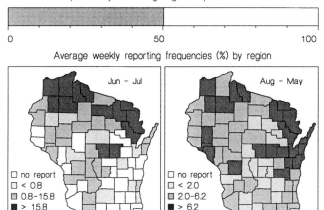

Average weekly reporting frequencies (%) during year

Changes in average weekly reporting frequencies (%) 1983-1996

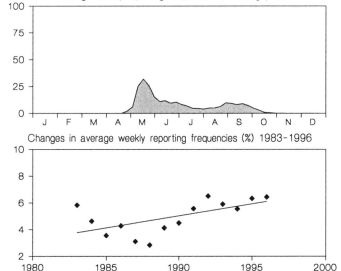

Northern Parula
Parula americana

Annual probability (%) of sighting this species in Wisconsin

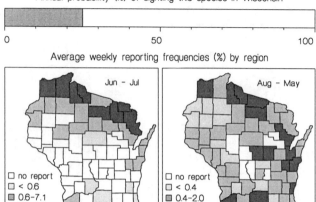

Average weekly reporting frequencies (%) by region

Jun – Jul

□ no report
□ < 0.6
▨ 0.6-7.1
■ > 7.1

Aug – May

□ no report
□ < 0.4
▨ 0.4-2.0
■ > 2.0

Average weekly reporting frequencies (%) during year

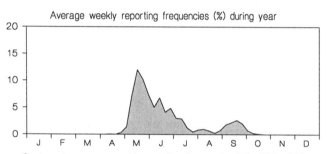

Changes in average weekly reporting frequencies (%) 1983-1996

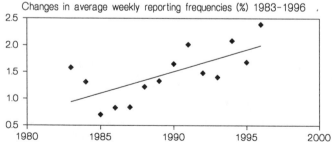

Yellow Warbler
Dendroica petechia

Annual probability (%) of sighting this species in Wisconsin

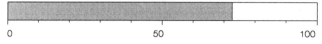

0	50	100

Average weekly reporting frequencies (%) by region

All Months

☐ no report
☐ < 7.3
▨ 7.3-14.0
■ > 14.0

Average weekly reporting frequencies (%) during year

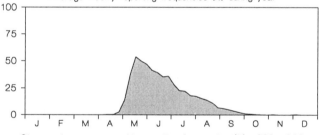

Changes in average weekly reporting frequencies (%) 1983-1996

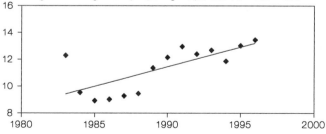

Chestnut-sided Warbler
Dendroica pensylvanica

Annual probability (%) of sighting this species in Wisconsin

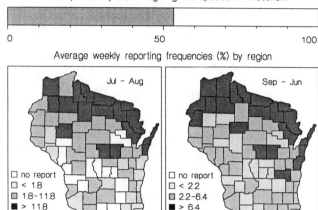

Average weekly reporting frequencies (%) by region

Jul – Aug

☐ no report
☐ < 1.8
▨ 1.8–11.8
■ > 11.8

Sep – Jun

☐ no report
☐ < 2.2
▨ 2.2–6.4
■ > 6.4

Average weekly reporting frequencies (%) during year

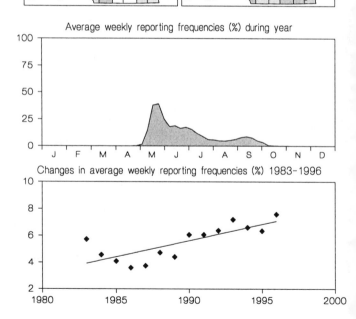

Changes in average weekly reporting frequencies (%) 1983–1996

Magnolia Warbler
Dendroica magnolia

Annual probability (%) of sighting this species in Wisconsin

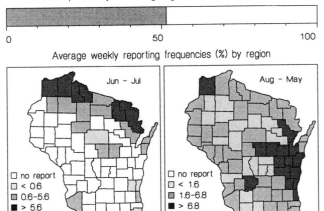

0   50   100

Average weekly reporting frequencies (%) by region

Jun – Jul

Aug – May

☐ no report
☐ < 0.6
▨ 0.6-5.6
■ > 5.6

☐ no report
☐ < 1.6
▨ 1.6-6.8
■ > 6.8

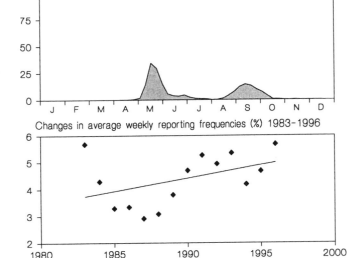

Average weekly reporting frequencies (%) during year

Changes in average weekly reporting frequencies (%) 1983-1996

Cape May Warbler
Dendroica tigrina

Annual probability (%) of sighting this species in Wisconsin

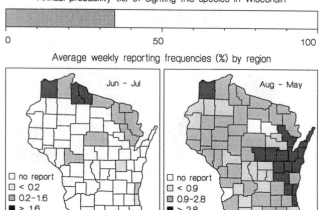

Average weekly reporting frequencies (%) by region

Jun – Jul

Aug – May

□ no report
□ < 0.2
▨ 0.2-1.6
■ > 1.6

□ no report
□ < 0.9
▨ 0.9-2.8
■ > 2.8

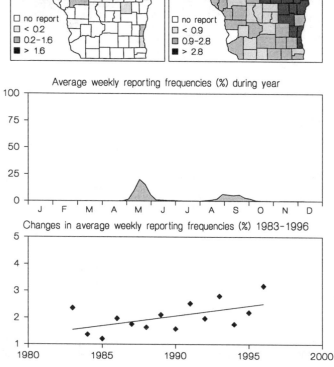

Average weekly reporting frequencies (%) during year

Changes in average weekly reporting frequencies (%) 1983-1996

Black-throated Blue Warbler
Dendroica caerulescens

Annual probability (%) of sighting this species in Wisconsin

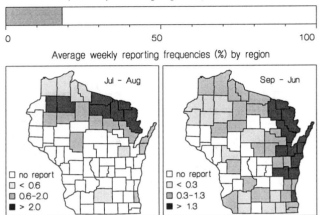

Average weekly reporting frequencies (%) by region

Jul – Aug

Sep – Jun

☐ no report
☐ < 0.6
▨ 0.6–2.0
■ > 2.0

☐ no report
☐ < 0.3
▨ 0.3–1.3
■ > 1.3

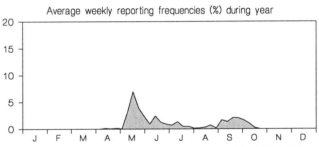

Average weekly reporting frequencies (%) during year

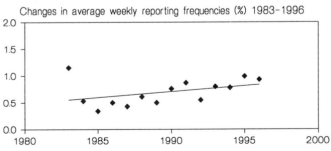

Changes in average weekly reporting frequencies (%) 1983–1996

Yellow-rumped Warbler
Dendroica coronata

Annual probability (%) of sighting this species in Wisconsin

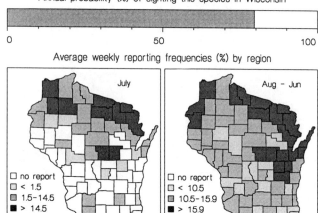

Average weekly reporting frequencies (%) by region

July

Aug - Jun

☐ no report
☐ < 1.5
▨ 1.5-14.5
■ > 14.5

☐ no report
☐ < 10.5
▨ 10.5-15.9
■ > 15.9

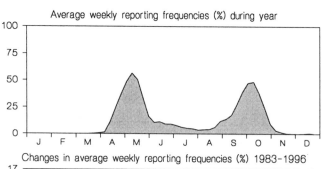

Average weekly reporting frequencies (%) during year

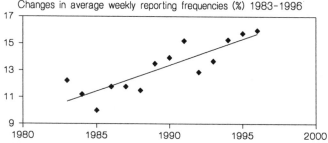

Changes in average weekly reporting frequencies (%) 1983-1996

Black-throated Green Warbler
Dendroica virens

Annual probability (%) of sighting this species in Wisconsin

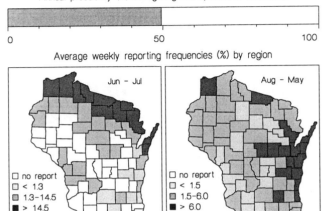

Average weekly reporting frequencies (%) by region

Jun – Jul

Aug – May

☐ no report
☐ < 1.3
▨ 1.3–14.5
■ > 14.5

☐ no report
☐ < 1.5
▨ 1.5–6.0
■ > 6.0

Average weekly reporting frequencies (%) during year

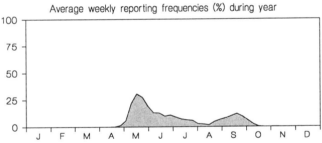

Changes in average weekly reporting frequencies (%) 1983-1996

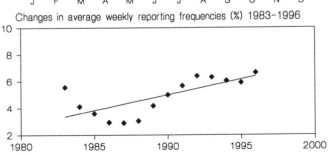

Blackburnian Warbler
Dendroica fusca

Annual probability (%) of sighting this species in Wisconsin

Average weekly reporting frequencies (%) by region

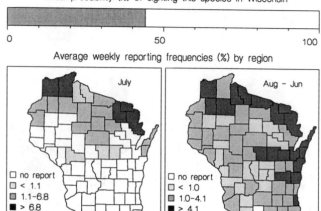

Average weekly reporting frequencies (%) during year

Changes in average weekly reporting frequencies (%) 1983-1996

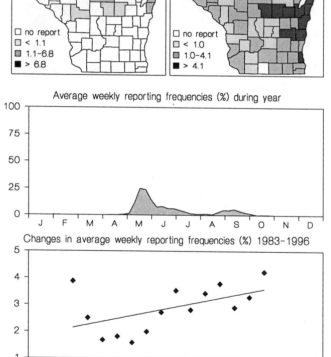

Pine Warbler
Dendroica pinus

Annual probability (%) of sighting this species in Wisconsin

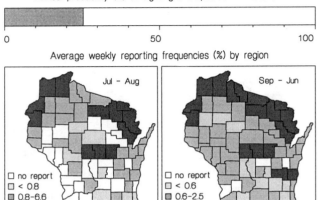

Average weekly reporting frequencies (%) by region

Jul – Aug

Sep – Jun

□ no report
□ < 0.8
▨ 0.8–6.6
■ > 6.6

□ no report
□ < 0.6
▨ 0.6–2.5
■ > 2.5

Average weekly reporting frequencies (%) during year

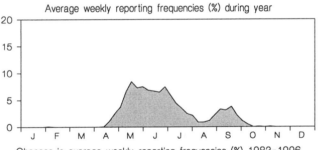

Changes in average weekly reporting frequencies (%) 1983–1996

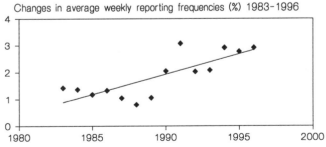

Palm Warbler
Dendroica palmarum

Annual probability (%) of sighting this species in Wisconsin

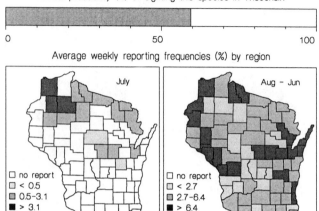

Average weekly reporting frequencies (%) by region

July

□ no report
□ < 0.5
▨ 0.5–3.1
■ > 3.1

Aug – Jun

□ no report
□ < 2.7
▨ 2.7–6.4
■ > 6.4

Average weekly reporting frequencies (%) during year

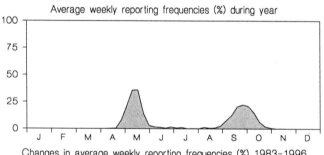

Changes in average weekly reporting frequencies (%) 1983–1996

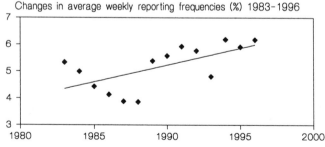

Bay-breasted Warbler
Dendroica castanea

Annual probability (%) of sighting this species in Wisconsin

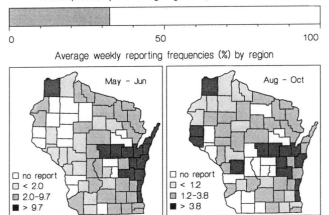

Average weekly reporting frequencies (%) by region

Average weekly reporting frequencies (%) during year

Changes in average weekly reporting frequencies (%) 1983-1996

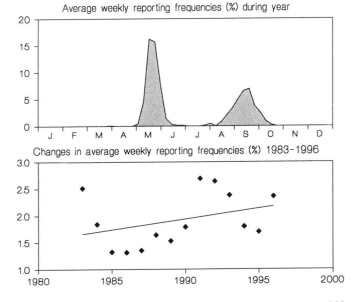

233

Blackpoll Warbler
Dendroica striata

Annual probability (%) of sighting this species in Wisconsin

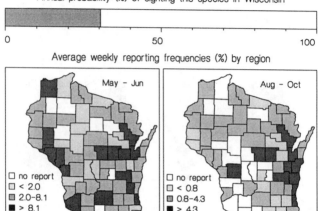

Average weekly reporting frequencies (%) by region

May – Jun

Aug – Oct

□ no report
□ < 2.0
▨ 2.0-8.1
■ > 8.1

□ no report
□ < 0.8
▨ 0.8-4.3
■ > 4.3

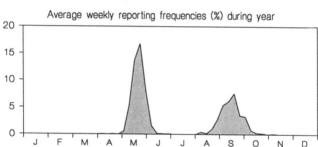

Average weekly reporting frequencies (%) during year

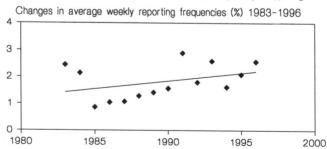

Changes in average weekly reporting frequencies (%) 1983-1996

Cerulean Warbler
Dendroica cerulea

Annual probability (%) of sighting this species in Wisconsin

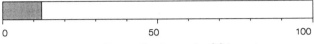

0   50   100

Average weekly reporting frequencies (%) by region

All Months

□ no report
□ < 0.2
▨ 0.2-0.8
■ > 0.8

Average weekly reporting frequencies (%) during year

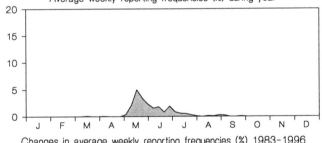

Changes in average weekly reporting frequencies (%) 1983-1996

Black-and-white Warbler
Mniotilta varia

Annual probability (%) of sighting this species in Wisconsin

0   50   100

Average weekly reporting frequencies (%) by region

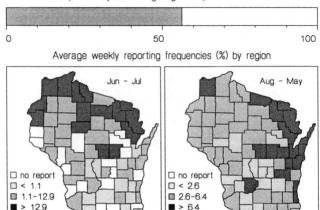

Jun – Jul

☐ no report
☐ < 1.1
▨ 1.1–12.9
■ > 12.9

Aug – May

☐ no report
☐ < 2.6
▨ 2.6–6.4
■ > 6.4

Average weekly reporting frequencies (%) during year

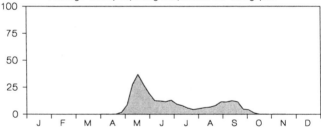

Changes in average weekly reporting frequencies (%) 1983-1996

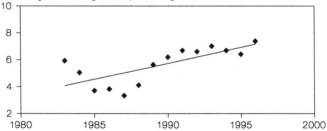

American Redstart
Setophaga ruticilla

Annual probability (%) of sighting this species in Wisconsin

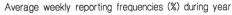

0   50   100

Average weekly reporting frequencies (%) by region

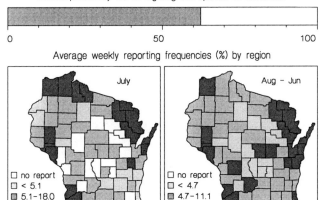

July

☐ no report
☐ < 5.1
▦ 5.1–18.0
■ > 18.0

Aug – Jun

☐ no report
☐ < 4.7
▦ 4.7–11.1
■ > 11.1

Average weekly reporting frequencies (%) during year

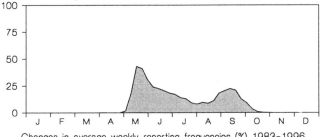

Changes in average weekly reporting frequencies (%) 1983–1996

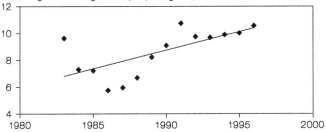

Prothonotary Warbler
Protonotaria citrea

Annual probability (%) of sighting this species in Wisconsin

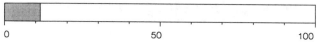

0   50   100

Average weekly reporting frequencies (%) by region

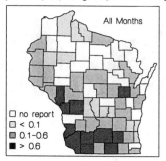

All Months

- □ no report
- ☐ < 0.1
- ▨ 0.1–0.6
- ■ > 0.6

Average weekly reporting frequencies (%) during year

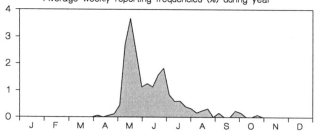

Changes in average weekly reporting frequencies (%) 1983–1996

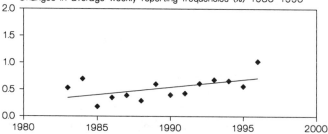

Ovenbird
Seiurus aurocapillus

Annual probability (%) of sighting this species in Wisconsin

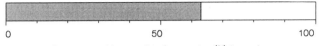

| 0 | 50 | 100 |

Average weekly reporting frequencies (%) by region

All Months

□ no report
□ < 5.2
▨ 5.2–13.2
■ > 13.2

Average weekly reporting frequencies (%) during year

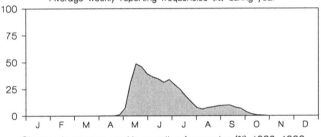

Changes in average weekly reporting frequencies (%) 1983–1996

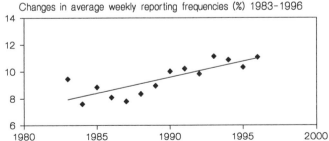

Northern Waterthrush
Seiurus noveboracensis

Annual probability (%) of sighting this species in Wisconsin

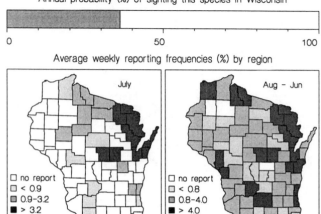

Average weekly reporting frequencies (%) by region

July

☐ no report
☐ < 0.9
▨ 0.9-3.2
■ > 3.2

Aug – Jun

☐ no report
☐ < 0.8
▨ 0.8-4.0
■ > 4.0

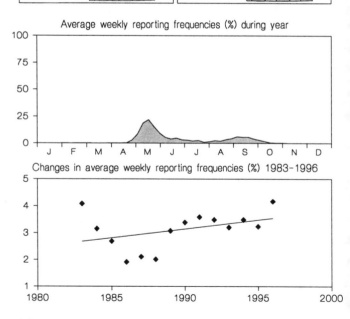

Average weekly reporting frequencies (%) during year

Changes in average weekly reporting frequencies (%) 1983-1996

Louisiana Waterthrush
Seiurus motacilla

Annual probability (%) of sighting this species in Wisconsin

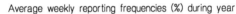

Average weekly reporting frequencies (%) by region

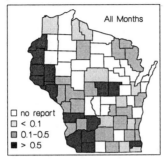

Average weekly reporting frequencies (%) during year

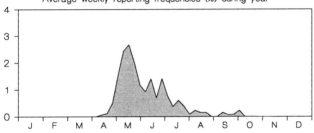

Changes in average weekly reporting frequencies (%) 1983–1996

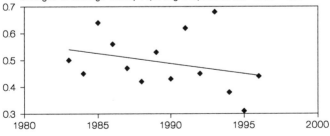

Kentucky Warbler
Oporornis formosus

Annual probability (%) of sighting this species in Wisconsin

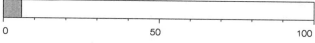

Average weekly reporting frequencies (%) by region

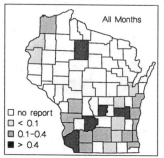

Average weekly reporting frequencies (%) during year

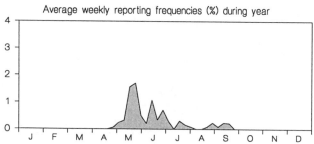

Changes in average weekly reporting frequencies (%) 1983–1996

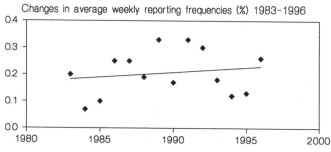

Connecticut Warbler
Oporornis agilis

Annual probability (%) of sighting this species in Wisconsin

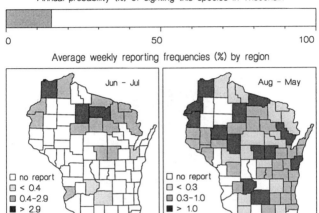

Average weekly reporting frequencies (%) by region

Jun – Jul

Aug – May

□ no report
□ < 0.4
▨ 0.4-2.9
■ > 2.9

□ no report
□ < 0.3
▨ 0.3-1.0
■ > 1.0

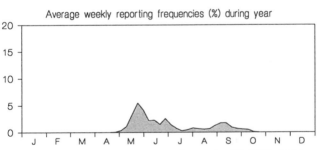

Average weekly reporting frequencies (%) during year

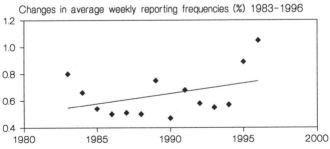

Changes in average weekly reporting frequencies (%) 1983-1996

Mourning Warbler
Oporornis philadelphia

Annual probability (%) of sighting this species in Wisconsin

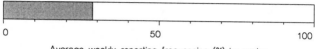

0	50	100

Average weekly reporting frequencies (%) by region

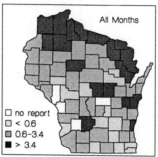

All Months

☐ no report
☐ < 0.6
▨ 0.6–3.4
■ > 3.4

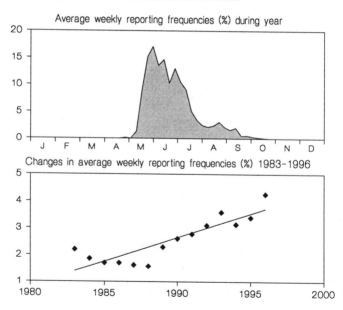

Average weekly reporting frequencies (%) during year

Changes in average weekly reporting frequencies (%) 1983–1996

Common Yellowthroat
Geothlypis trichas

Annual probability (%) of sighting this species in Wisconsin

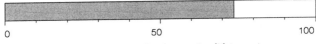

0   50   100

Average weekly reporting frequencies (%) by region

All Months

☐ no report
☐ < 12.4
▨ 12.4–21.1
■ > 21.1

Average weekly reporting frequencies (%) during year

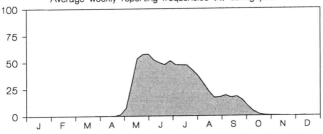

Changes in average weekly reporting frequencies (%) 1983–1996

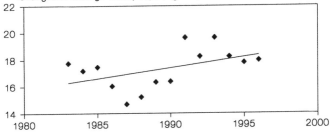

Hooded Warbler
Wilsonia citrina

Annual probability (%) of sighting this species in Wisconsin

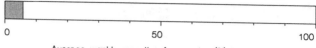

0   50   100

Average weekly reporting frequencies (%) by region

All Months

☐ no report
☐ < 0.1
▨ 0.1–0.5
■ > 0.5

Average weekly reporting frequencies (%) during year

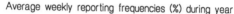
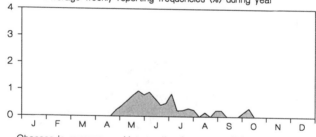

Changes in average weekly reporting frequencies (%) 1983–1996

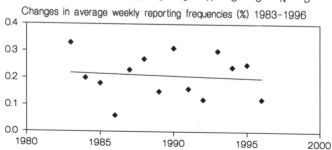

Wilson's Warbler
Wilsonia pusilla

Annual probability (%) of sighting this species in Wisconsin

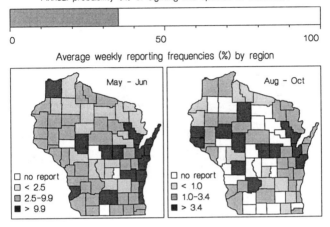

Average weekly reporting frequencies (%) by region

Average weekly reporting frequencies (%) during year

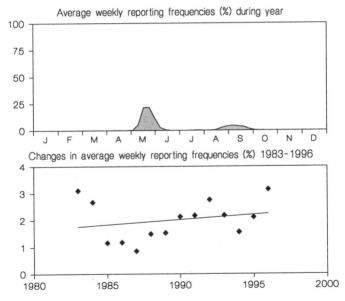

Changes in average weekly reporting frequencies (%) 1983-1996

Canada Warbler
Wilsonia canadensis

Annual probability (%) of sighting this species in Wisconsin

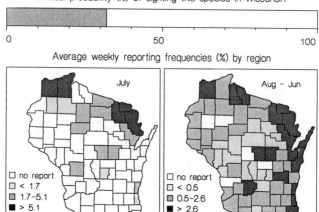

Average weekly reporting frequencies (%) by region

July

Aug – Jun

□ no report
□ < 1.7
▨ 1.7–5.1
■ > 5.1

□ no report
□ < 0.5
▨ 0.5–2.6
■ > 2.6

Average weekly reporting frequencies (%) during year

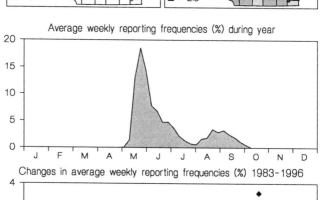

Changes in average weekly reporting frequencies (%) 1983–1996

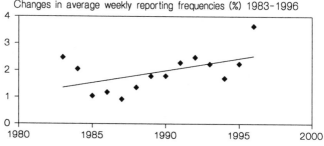

Yellow-breasted Chat
Icteria virens

Annual probability (%) of sighting this species in Wisconsin

0   50   100

Average weekly reporting frequencies (%) by region

All Months

☐ no report
☐ < 0.1
▨ 0.1–0.4
■ > 0.4

Average weekly reporting frequencies (%) during year

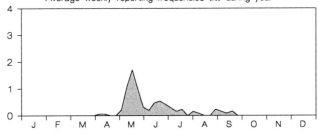

Changes in average weekly reporting frequencies (%) 1983–1996

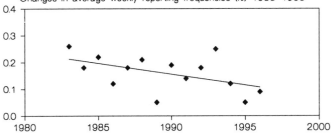

Scarlet Tanager
Piranga olivacea

Annual probability (%) of sighting this species in Wisconsin

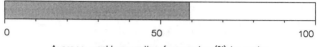

| 0 | 50 | 100 |

Average weekly reporting frequencies (%) by region

All Months

□ no report
□ < 3.5
▨ 3.5–8.0
■ > 8.0

Average weekly reporting frequencies (%) during year

Changes in average weekly reporting frequencies (%) 1983–1996

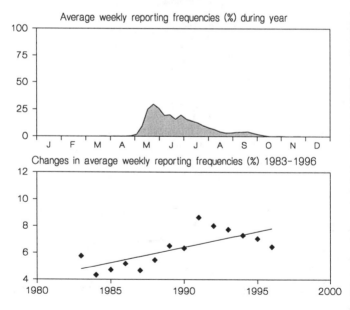

Northern Cardinal
Cardinalis cardinalis

Annual probability (%) of sighting this species in Wisconsin

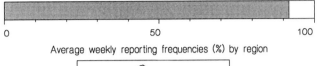

0   50   100

Average weekly reporting frequencies (%) by region

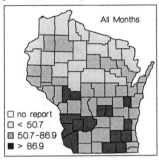

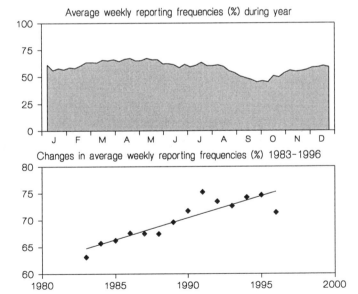

Average weekly reporting frequencies (%) during year

Changes in average weekly reporting frequencies (%) 1983-1996

Rose-breasted Grosbeak
Pheucticus ludovicianus

Annual probability (%) of sighting this species in Wisconsin

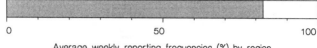

0   50   100

Average weekly reporting frequencies (%) by region

All Months

☐ no report
☐ < 13.3
▨ 13.3-26.2
■ > 26.2

Average weekly reporting frequencies (%) during year

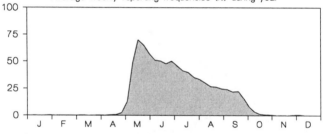

Changes in average weekly reporting frequencies (%) 1983-1996

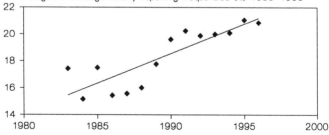

Indigo Bunting
Passerina cyanea

Annual probability (%) of sighting this species in Wisconsin

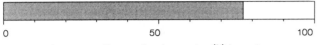

0   50   100

Average weekly reporting frequencies (%) by region

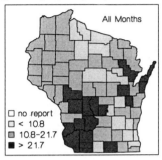

All Months

- ☐ no report
- ☐ < 10.8
- ▨ 10.8-21.7
- ■ > 21.7

Average weekly reporting frequencies (%) during year

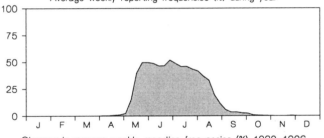

Changes in average weekly reporting frequencies (%) 1983-1996

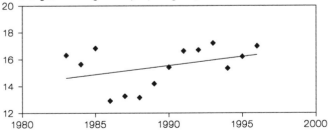

Dickcissel
Spiza americana

Annual probability (%) of sighting this species in Wisconsin

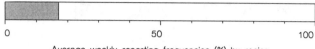

0   50   100

Average weekly reporting frequencies (%) by region

All Months

☐ no report
☐ < 0.4
▨ 0.4–1.8
■ > 1.8

Average weekly reporting frequencies (%) during year

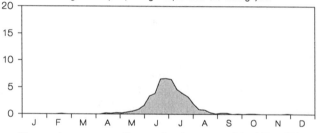

Changes in average weekly reporting frequencies (%) 1983–1996

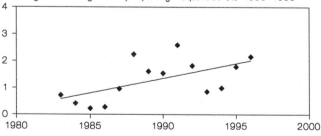

Eastern Towhee
Pipilo erythrophthalmus

Annual probability (%) of sighting this species in Wisconsin

0	50	100

Average weekly reporting frequencies (%) by region

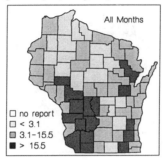

All Months

□ no report
□ < 3.1
▨ 3.1–15.5
■ > 15.5

Average weekly reporting frequencies (%) during year

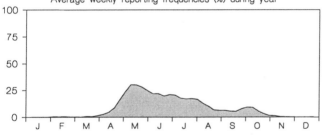

Changes in average weekly reporting frequencies (%) 1983–1996

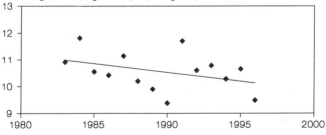

American Tree Sparrow
Spizella arborea

Annual probability (%) of sighting this species in Wisconsin

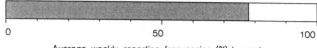

Average weekly reporting frequencies (%) by region

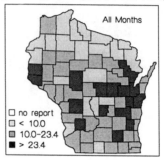

All Months

□ no report
□ < 10.0
▨ 10.0-23.4
■ > 23.4

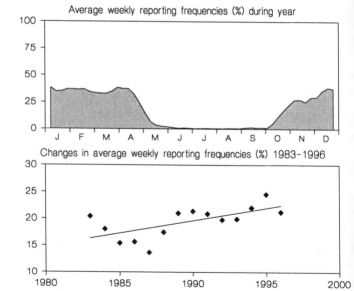

Average weekly reporting frequencies (%) during year

Changes in average weekly reporting frequencies (%) 1983-1996

Chipping Sparrow
Spizella passerina

Annual probability (%) of sighting this species in Wisconsin

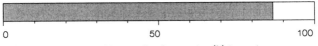

0   50   100

Average weekly reporting frequencies (%) by region

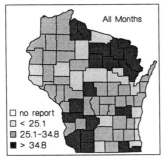

All Months

□ no report
□ < 25.1
▨ 25.1–34.8
■ > 34.8

Average weekly reporting frequencies (%) during year

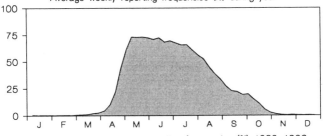

Changes in average weekly reporting frequencies (%) 1983–1996

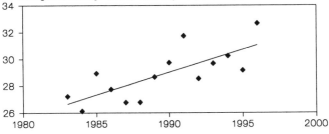

Clay-colored Sparrow
Spizella pallida

Annual probability (%) of sighting this species in Wisconsin

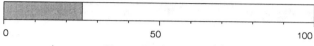

| 0 | 50 | 100 |

Average weekly reporting frequencies (%) by region

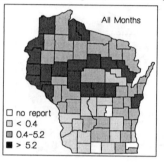

All Months

- □ no report
- □ < 0.4
- ▨ 0.4–5.2
- ■ > 5.2

Average weekly reporting frequencies (%) during year

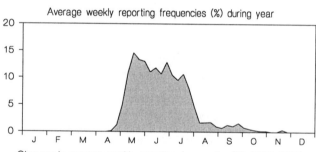

Changes in average weekly reporting frequencies (%) 1983-1996

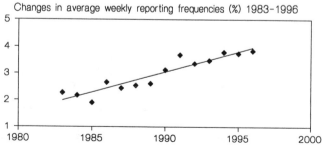

Field Sparrow
Spizella pusilla

Annual probability (%) of sighting this species in Wisconsin

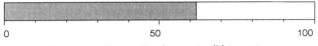

0	50	100

Average weekly reporting frequencies (%) by region

All Months

- □ no report
- □ < 4.0
- ▨ 4.0-20.4
- ■ > 20.4

Average weekly reporting frequencies (%) during year

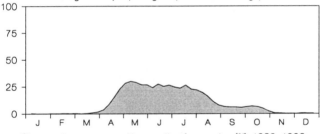

Changes in average weekly reporting frequencies (%) 1983-1996

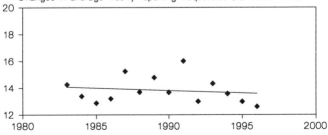

Vesper Sparrow
Pooecetes gramineus

Annual probability (%) of sighting this species in Wisconsin

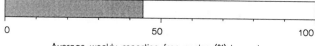

| 0 | 50 | 100 |

Average weekly reporting frequencies (%) by region

All Months

□ no report
▨ < 2.1
▨ 2.1–11.5
■ > 11.5

Average weekly reporting frequencies (%) during year

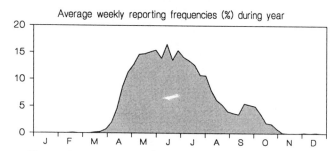

Changes in average weekly reporting frequencies (%) 1983–1996

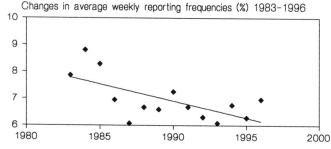

Lark Sparrow
Chondestes grammacus

Annual probability (%) of sighting this species in Wisconsin

0   50   100

Average weekly reporting frequencies (%) by region

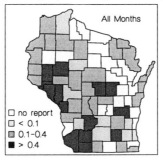

All Months

☐ no report
☐ < 0.1
▨ 0.1–0.4
■ > 0.4

Average weekly reporting frequencies (%) during year

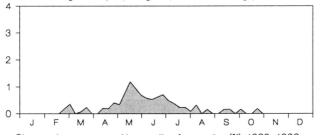

Changes in average weekly reporting frequencies (%) 1983–1996

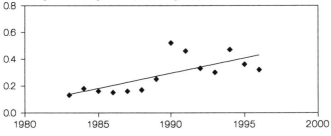

Savannah Sparrow
Passerculus sandwichensis

Annual probability (%) of sighting this species in Wisconsin

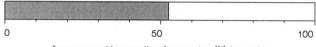

Average weekly reporting frequencies (%) by region

All Months

□ no report
□ < 3.5
▨ 3.5–15.2
■ > 15.2

Average weekly reporting frequencies (%) during year

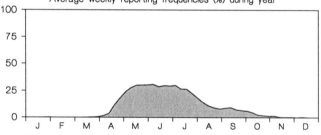

Changes in average weekly reporting frequencies (%) 1983–1996

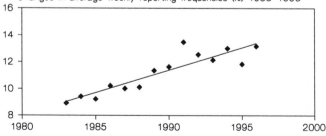

Grasshopper Sparrow
Ammodramus savannarum

Annual probability (%) of sighting this species in Wisconsin

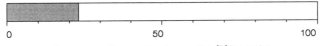

0	50	100

Average weekly reporting frequencies (%) by region

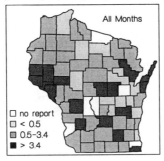

All Months

□ no report
□ < 0.5
▦ 0.5-3.4
■ > 3.4

Average weekly reporting frequencies (%) during year

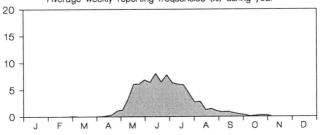

Changes in average weekly reporting frequencies (%) 1983-1996

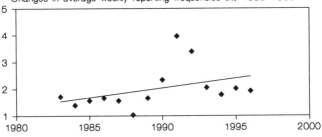

Henslow's Sparrow
Ammodramus henslowii

Annual probability (%) of sighting this species in Wisconsin

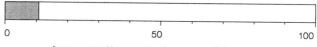

| 0 | 50 | 100 |

Average weekly reporting frequencies (%) by region

All Months

☐ no report
☐ < 0.2
▨ 0.2–0.9
■ > 0.9

Average weekly reporting frequencies (%) during year

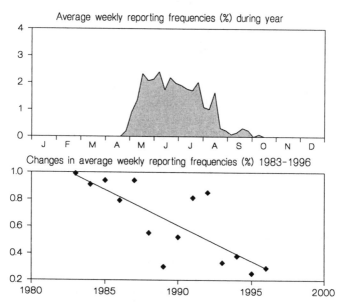

Changes in average weekly reporting frequencies (%) 1983–1996

Le Conte's Sparrow
Ammodramus leconteii

Annual probability (%) of sighting this species in Wisconsin

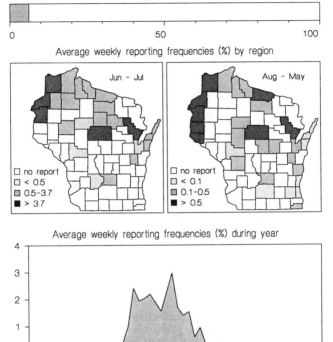

Average weekly reporting frequencies (%) by region

Jun – Jul

Aug – May

□ no report
□ < 0.5
▨ 0.5–3.7
■ > 3.7

□ no report
□ < 0.1
▨ 0.1–0.5
■ > 0.5

Average weekly reporting frequencies (%) during year

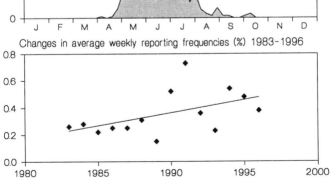

Changes in average weekly reporting frequencies (%) 1983–1996

Fox Sparrow
Passerella iliaca

Annual probability (%) of sighting this species in Wisconsin

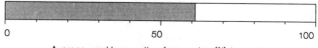

| 0 | 50 | 100 |

Average weekly reporting frequencies (%) by region

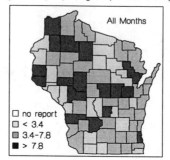

All Months

□ no report
□ < 3.4
▦ 3.4–7.8
■ > 7.8

Average weekly reporting frequencies (%) during year

Changes in average weekly reporting frequencies (%) 1983–1996

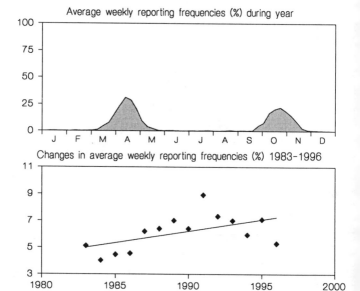

Song Sparrow
Melospiza melodia

Annual probability (%) of sighting this species in Wisconsin

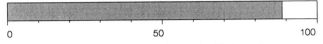

0   50   100

Average weekly reporting frequencies (%) by region

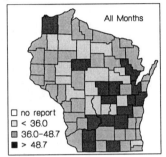

Average weekly reporting frequencies (%) during year

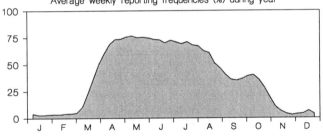

Changes in average weekly reporting frequencies (%) 1983-1996

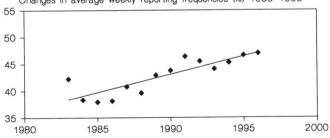

267

Lincoln's Sparrow
Melospiza lincolnii

Annual probability (%) of sighting this species in Wisconsin

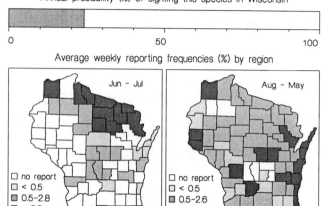

Average weekly reporting frequencies (%) by region

Jun – Jul

□ no report
□ < 0.5
▨ 0.5–2.8
■ > 2.8

Aug – May

□ no report
□ < 0.5
▨ 0.5–2.6
■ > 2.6

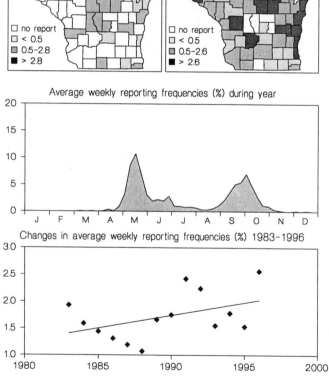

Average weekly reporting frequencies (%) during year

Changes in average weekly reporting frequencies (%) 1983–1996

Swamp Sparrow
Melospiza georgiana

Annual probability (%) of sighting this species in Wisconsin

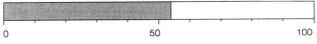

Average weekly reporting frequencies (%) by region

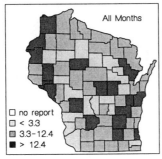

All Months

☐ no report
☐ < 3.3
▨ 3.3–12.4
■ > 12.4

Average weekly reporting frequencies (%) during year

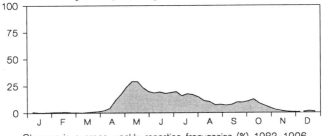

Changes in average weekly reporting frequencies (%) 1983–1996

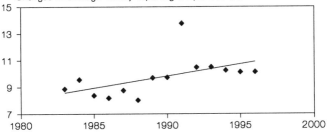

White-throated Sparrow
Zonotrichia albicollis

Annual probability (%) of sighting this species in Wisconsin

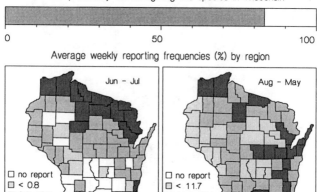

Average weekly reporting frequencies (%) by region

Jun – Jul

□ no report
□ < 0.8
▨ 0.8–16.8
■ > 16.8

Aug – May

□ no report
□ < 11.7
▨ 11.7–20.4
■ > 20.4

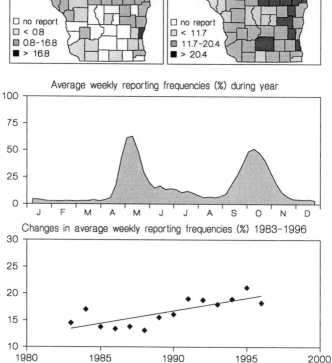

Average weekly reporting frequencies (%) during year

Changes in average weekly reporting frequencies (%) 1983–1996

White-crowned Sparrow
Zonotrichia leucophrys

Annual probability (%) of sighting this species in Wisconsin

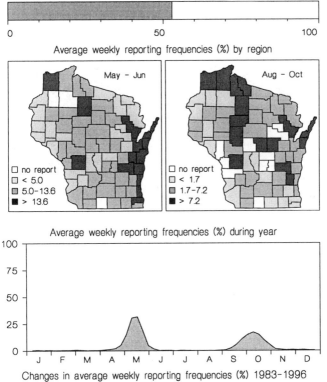

Average weekly reporting frequencies (%) by region

May – Jun

□ no report
□ < 5.0
▨ 5.0-13.6
■ > 13.6

Aug – Oct

□ no report
□ < 1.7
▨ 1.7-7.2
■ > 7.2

Average weekly reporting frequencies (%) during year

Changes in average weekly reporting frequencies (%) 1983-1996

Harris' Sparrow
Zonotrichia querula

Annual probability (%) of sighting this species in Wisconsin

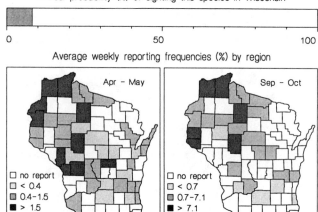

Average weekly reporting frequencies (%) by region

Apr – May

Sep – Oct

□ no report
□ < 0.4
▦ 0.4–1.5
■ > 1.5

□ no report
□ < 0.7
▦ 0.7–7.1
■ > 7.1

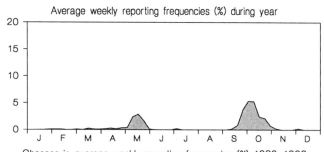

Average weekly reporting frequencies (%) during year

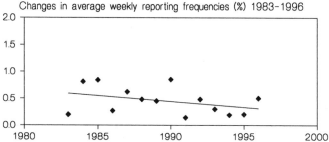

Changes in average weekly reporting frequencies (%) 1983–1996

Dark-eyed Junco
Junco hyemalis

Annual probability (%) of sighting this species in Wisconsin

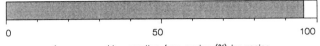

Average weekly reporting frequencies (%) by region

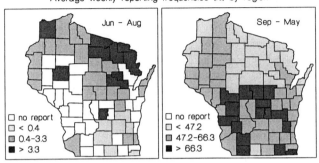

Average weekly reporting frequencies (%) during year

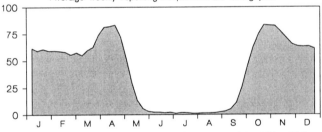

Changes in average weekly reporting frequencies (%) 1983-1996

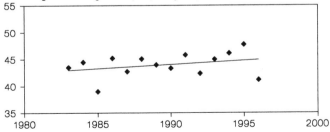

Lapland Longspur
Calcarius lapponicus

Annual probability (%) of sighting this species in Wisconsin

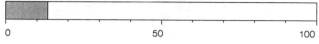

0	50	100

Average weekly reporting frequencies (%) by region

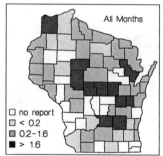

All Months

□ no report
< 0.2
0.2–1.6
■ > 1.6

Average weekly reporting frequencies (%) during year

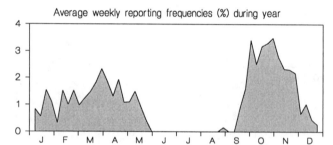

Changes in average weekly reporting frequencies (%) 1983–1996

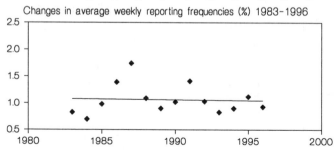

Snow Bunting
Plectrophenax nivalis

Annual probability (%) of sighting this species in Wisconsin

| 0 | 50 | 100 |

Average weekly reporting frequencies (%) by region

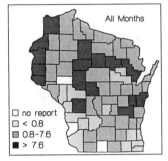

All Months

- □ no report
- □ < 0.8
- ▨ 0.8–7.6
- ■ > 7.6

Average weekly reporting frequencies (%) during year

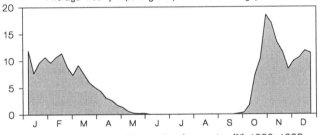

Changes in average weekly reporting frequencies (%) 1983–1996

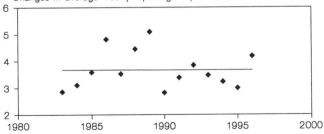

Bobolink
Dolichonyx oryzivorus

Annual probability (%) of sighting this species in Wisconsin

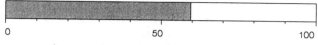

| 0 | 50 | 100 |

Average weekly reporting frequencies (%) by region

All Months

□ no report
□ < 4.7
▨ 4.7–11.6
■ > 11.6

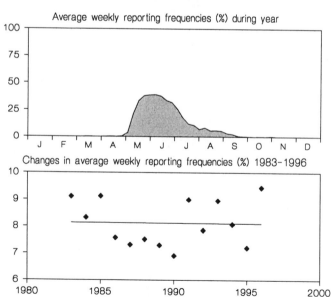

Average weekly reporting frequencies (%) during year

Changes in average weekly reporting frequencies (%) 1983–1996

Red-winged Blackbird
Agelaius phoeniceus

Annual probability (%) of sighting this species in Wisconsin

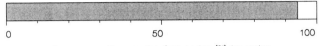

0   50   100

Average weekly reporting frequencies (%) by region

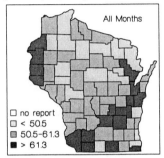

All Months

☐ no report
☐ < 50.5
▨ 50.5-61.3
■ > 61.3

Average weekly reporting frequencies (%) during year

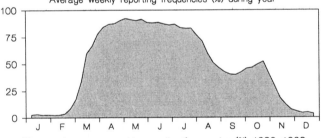

Changes in average weekly reporting frequencies (%) 1983-1996

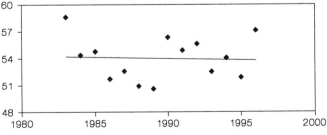

Eastern Meadowlark
Sturnella magna

Annual probability (%) of sighting this species in Wisconsin

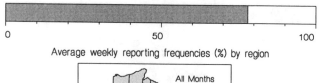

| 0 | 50 | 100 |

Average weekly reporting frequencies (%) by region

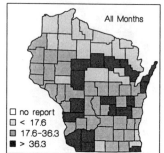

All Months

□ no report
□ < 17.6
▨ 17.6-36.3
■ > 36.3

Average weekly reporting frequencies (%) during year

Changes in average weekly reporting frequencies (%) 1983-1996

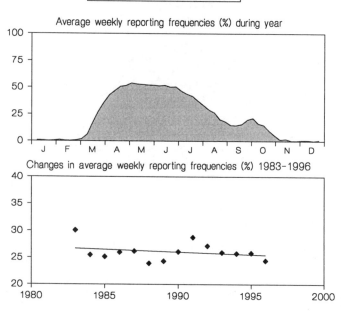

Western Meadowlark
Sturnella neglecta

Annual probability (%) of sighting this species in Wisconsin

| 0 | 50 | 100 |

Average weekly reporting frequencies (%) by region

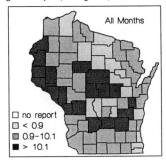

All Months

- ☐ no report
- ☐ < 0.9
- ▨ 0.9–10.1
- ■ > 10.1

Average weekly reporting frequencies (%) during year

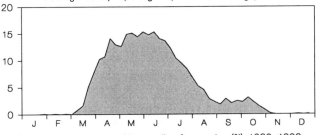

Changes in average weekly reporting frequencies (%) 1983–1996

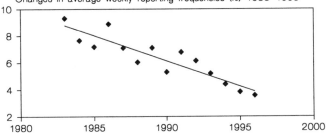

Yellow-headed Blackbird
Xanthocephalus xanthocephalus

Annual probability (%) of sighting this species in Wisconsin

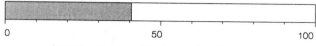

Average weekly reporting frequencies (%) by region

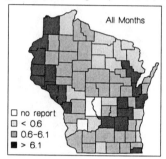

All Months

□ no report
□ < 0.6
▨ 0.6-6.1
■ > 6.1

Average weekly reporting frequencies (%) during year

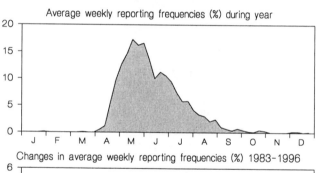

Changes in average weekly reporting frequencies (%) 1983-1996

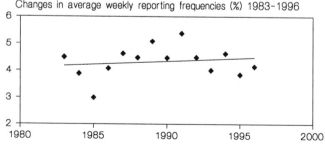

Rusty Blackbird
Euphagus carolinus

Annual probability (%) of sighting this species in Wisconsin

| 0 | 50 | 100 |

Average weekly reporting frequencies (%) by region

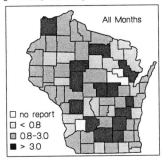

All Months

☐ no report
☐ < 0.8
▨ 0.8–3.0
■ > 3.0

Average weekly reporting frequencies (%) during year

Changes in average weekly reporting frequencies (%) 1983–1996

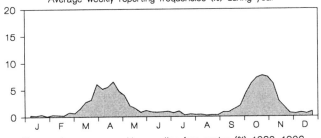

Brewer's Blackbird
Euphagus cyanocephalus

Annual probability (%) of sighting this species in Wisconsin

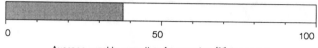

0	50	100

Average weekly reporting frequencies (%) by region

All Months

□ no report
□ < 2.0
▨ 2.0–9.5
■ > 9.5

Average weekly reporting frequencies (%) during year

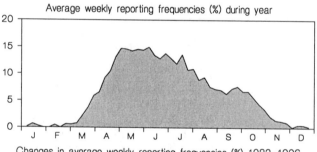

Changes in average weekly reporting frequencies (%) 1983–1996

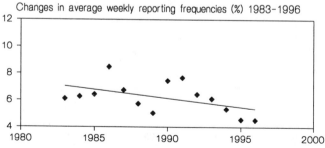

Common Grackle
Quiscalus quiscula

Annual probability (%) of sighting this species in Wisconsin

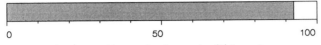

| 0 | 50 | 100 |

Average weekly reporting frequencies (%) by region

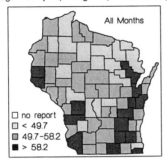

All Months

- □ no report
- □ < 49.7
- ▨ 49.7–58.2
- ■ > 58.2

Average weekly reporting frequencies (%) during year

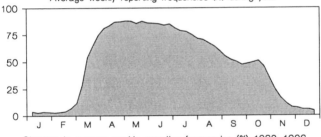

Changes in average weekly reporting frequencies (%) 1983–1996

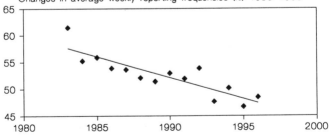

Brown-headed Cowbird
Molothrus ater

Annual probability (%) of sighting this species in Wisconsin

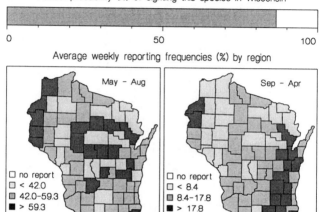

Average weekly reporting frequencies (%) by region

May – Aug

Sep – Apr

□ no report
□ < 42.0
▨ 42.0–59.3
■ > 59.3

□ no report
□ < 8.4
▨ 8.4–17.8
■ > 17.8

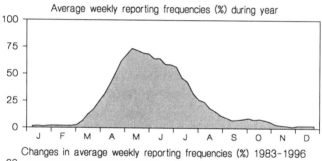

Average weekly reporting frequencies (%) during year

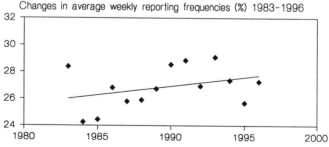

Changes in average weekly reporting frequencies (%) 1983–1996

Orchard Oriole
Icterus spurius

Annual probability (%) of sighting this species in Wisconsin

0 50 100

Average weekly reporting frequencies (%) by region

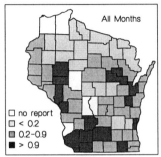

All Months

☐ no report
☐ < 0.2
▨ 0.2–0.9
■ > 0.9

Average weekly reporting frequencies (%) during year

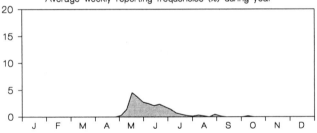

Changes in average weekly reporting frequencies (%) 1983–1996

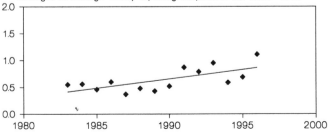

Baltimore Oriole
Icterus galbula

Annual probability (%) of sighting this species in Wisconsin

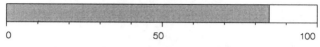

0   50   100

Average weekly reporting frequencies (%) by region

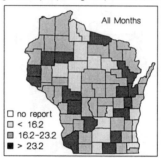

All Months

☐ no report
☐ < 16.2
▨ 16.2–23.2
■ > 23.2

Average weekly reporting frequencies (%) during year

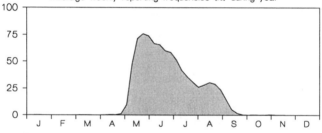

Changes in average weekly reporting frequencies (%) 1983–1996

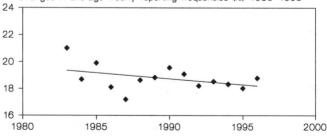

Pine Grosbeak
Pinicola enucleator

Annual probability (%) of sighting this species in Wisconsin

| 0 | 50 | 100 |

Average weekly reporting frequencies (%) by region

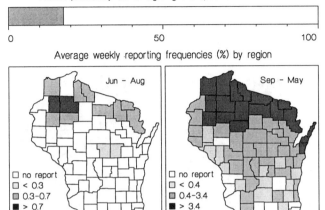

Average weekly reporting frequencies (%) during year

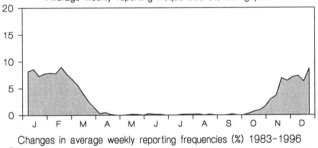

Changes in average weekly reporting frequencies (%) 1983-1996

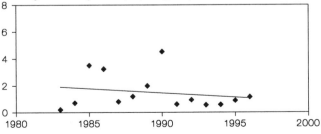

Purple Finch
Carpodacus purpureus

Annual probability (%) of sighting this species in Wisconsin

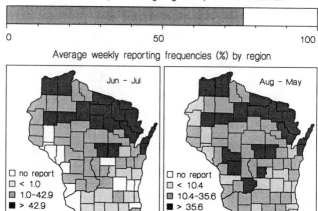

Average weekly reporting frequencies (%) by region

Jun – Jul

☐ no report
☐ < 1.0
▨ 1.0–42.9
■ > 42.9

Aug – May

☐ no report
☐ < 10.4
▨ 10.4–35.6
■ > 35.6

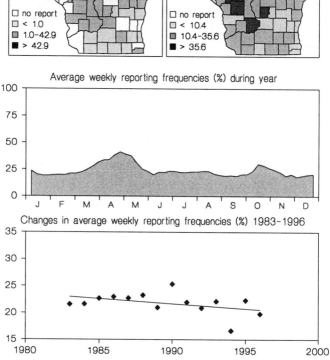

Average weekly reporting frequencies (%) during year

Changes in average weekly reporting frequencies (%) 1983–1996

House Finch
Carpodacus mexicanus

Annual probability (%) of sighting this species in Wisconsin

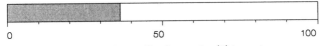

| 0 | 50 | 100 |

Average weekly reporting frequencies (%) by region

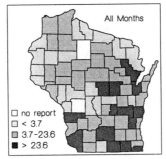

All Months

☐ no report
☐ < 3.7
▨ 3.7–23.6
■ > 23.6

Average weekly reporting frequencies (%) during year

Changes in average weekly reporting frequencies (%) 1991–1996

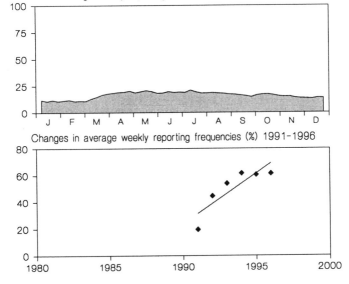

Red Crossbill
Loxia curvirostra

Annual probability (%) of sighting this species in Wisconsin

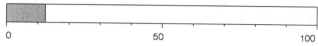

0   50   100

Average weekly reporting frequencies (%) by region

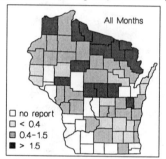

All Months

□ no report
□ < 0.4
▨ 0.4–1.5
■ > 1.5

Average weekly reporting frequencies (%) during year

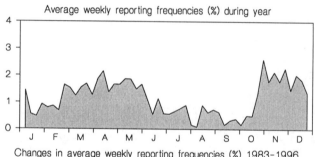

Changes in average weekly reporting frequencies (%) 1983–1996

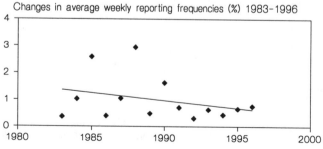

White-winged Crossbill
Loxia leucoptera

Annual probability (%) of sighting this species in Wisconsin

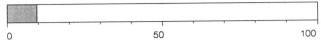

0   50   100

Average weekly reporting frequencies (%) by region

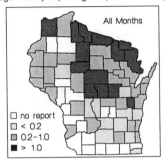

All Months

□ no report
□ < 0.2
▨ 0.2-1.0
■ > 1.0

Average weekly reporting frequencies (%) during year

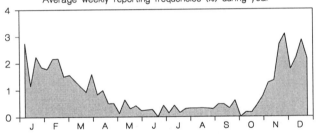

Changes in average weekly reporting frequencies (%) 1983-1996

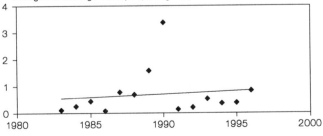

Common Redpoll
Carduelis flammea

Annual probability (%) of sighting this species in Wisconsin

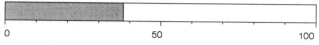

| 0 | 50 | 100 |

Average weekly reporting frequencies (%) by region

All Months

□ no report
□ < 1.1
▨ 1.1–9.4
■ > 9.4

Average weekly reporting frequencies (%) during year

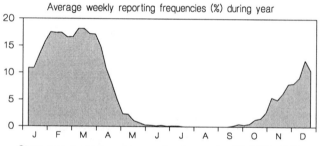

Changes in average weekly reporting frequencies (%) 1983–1996

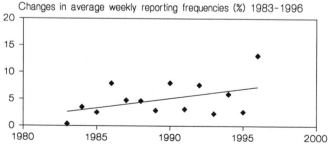

Pine Siskin
Carduelis pinus

Annual probability (%) of sighting this species in Wisconsin

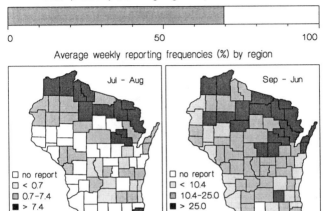

Average weekly reporting frequencies (%) by region

Jul – Aug

Sep – Jun

□ no report
□ < 0.7
▨ 0.7-7.4
■ > 7.4

□ no report
□ < 10.4
▨ 10.4-25.0
■ > 25.0

Average weekly reporting frequencies (%) during year

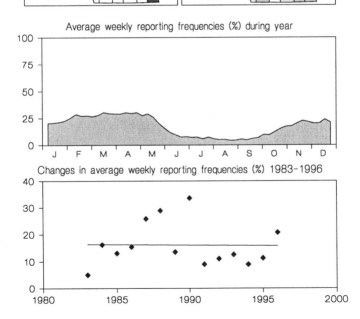

Changes in average weekly reporting frequencies (%) 1983-1996

American Goldfinch
Carduelis tristis

Annual probability (%) of sighting this species in Wisconsin

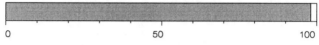

Average weekly reporting frequencies (%) by region

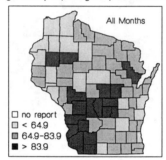

Average weekly reporting frequencies (%) during year

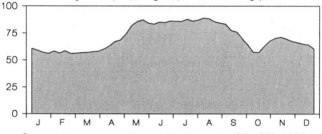

Changes in average weekly reporting frequencies (%) 1983-1996

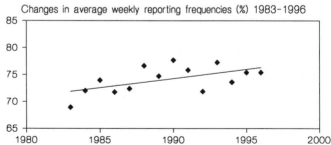

Evening Grosbeak
Coccothraustes vespertinus

Annual probability (%) of sighting this species in Wisconsin

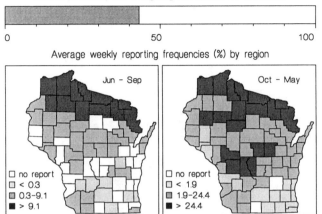

Average weekly reporting frequencies (%) by region

Jun – Sep

Oct – May

□ no report
□ < 0.3
▨ 0.3-9.1
■ > 9.1

□ no report
□ < 1.9
▨ 1.9-24.4
■ > 24.4

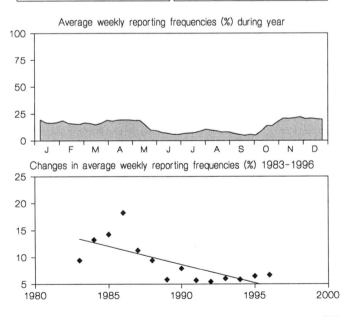

Average weekly reporting frequencies (%) during year

Changes in average weekly reporting frequencies (%) 1983-1996

House Sparrow
Passer domesticus

Annual probability (%) of sighting this species in Wisconsin

0   50   100

Average weekly reporting frequencies (%) by region

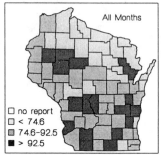

All Months

☐ no report
☐ < 74.6
▨ 74.6–92.5
■ > 92.5

Average weekly reporting frequencies (%) during year

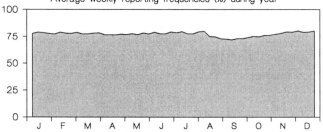

Changes in average weekly reporting frequencies (%) 1983–1996

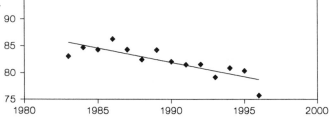

Appendix

THE WISCONSIN CHECKLIST PROJECT

Only a few American birdwatchers ever participate in an organized program for monitoring bird populations, such as the North American Breeding Bird Survey (Bystrak 1981), North American Nest-Record Card Program (Peakall 1970), Colonial Bird Register (McCrimmon 1977), Audubon Breeding-Bird Census (Hall 1964), Audubon Winter Bird-Population Study (Robbins 1981), or various bird atlas projects in individual states (Robbins 1977). Many of them, nonetheless, regularly document their birding activities by recording their findings on checklists.

A checklist is a simple record of the species of birds the field observer found at a particular place and time. This form of record-keeping has long been a standard activity among American birdwatchers (Hickey 1943). Checklists have been an overlooked and underrated source of information on bird populations. In fact, checklist records of a single observer are by themselves of limited value in monitoring bird populations. But when the collective checklists of many individual observers are combined and analyzed properly, they can yield a surprising variety of information on bird populations (Temple 1996).

Temple and Temple (1976) were among the first to explore the potential value of checklist records in monitoring bird populations. In theory, there are several types of information on bird populations that can be derived from checklist data (Temple 1981).

When many observers in an area keep concurrent checklist records, their checklists will differ. Some species will be reported on every observer's checklist, whereas other species will occur on those of only a few observers. The reporting frequency for each species in an area can be calculated as the percentage of checklists on which the species had been reported. Reporting frequencies for a species are correlated with its abundance in an area at a particular time (see Temple and Temple 1986). A high reporting frequency indicates that a species is relatively abundant, whereas a low reporting frequency indicates that a species is relatively uncommon.

When checklist records are kept by many observers over a wide geographical area, the occurrence of a species on a checklist from a specific locality confirms the presence of the species there. A map of the localities where a species has been reported reveals the geographical range of the species. Geographical patterns in reporting frequencies reflect geographical patterns of relative abundance (Temple and Temple 1986).

If checklist records are kept regularly during the year, the seasonal distribution of checklist reports reveals the presence or absence of each species in a particular locality at various times throughout the year. Seasonal patterns in reporting frequencies reflect the changing abundance of a species throughout the year and reveal how the abundance changes as a result of migratory ovements, reproduction, and mortality (Temple and Temple 1984). The patterns revealed by the checklist records can, for example, reflect a migratory movements of a species to and from an area (Temple and Cary 1987).

Over many years, changes in reporting frequencies can reveal long-term changes in the abundance and distribution of a species. Year-to-year changes in reporting frequencies are to be expected, but for some species there will be a trend. Increasing, decreasing, and cyclic patterns can alert us to how a population is changing over time and can trigger the search for an explanation.

This book presents the results of a project, now in its sixteenth year (1982–97), designed to demonstrate that an analysis of checklist records provided by birdwatchers can produce useful information about bird populations in Wisconsin. The Wisconsin Checklist Project is one of the most ambitious attempts to explore the full potential of checklist records. Because the project involves such a novel approach to monitoring bird populations, we describe it here in some detail, so that both the methods and the results of the project can be fairly evaluated.

The first and most important requirement for a project of this type is a group of competent birdwatchers who are willing to cooperate in a voluntary research effort. We were fortunate, indeed, that such a group of field observers exists in Wisconsin. The Wisconsin Society for Ornithology, with some 1200 enthusiastic and skillful members, has had a long tradition of volunteer participation in research programs in the state. In response to the call for participants (Temple 1982), 230 WSO members contributed to the checklist project during its first year, and approximately 100 participants have contributed each year since then. This impressive rate of participation no doubt reflects the attractiveness of this simple approach to record-keeping.

We asked participants to keep careful records of the bird species that they had detected during each week of the year, and we provided them with special forms on which to record information for each week. These forms were designed so that the information recorded on them could be read directly by an optical scanning device; this innovation made it possible for us to transfer large amounts of information rapidly and easily from the forms to magnetic tapes and disks that could then be used by computers.

On the weekly forms, participants identified themselves and provided information on the county in which they had birded during the recording week, the date of the Sunday that began the recording week, and the species of birds they had detected. A sample of the recording form is printed on pages 304–305.

Before continuing with the analysis of these data, we tried to identify and correct any obvious errors made by participants. Although errors were uncommon, typical examples included incorrect spelling of the reporter's name, incorrect dates for the start of a week, and nonexistent county identification codes. Such errors could, of course, be easily detected and corrected.

We also examined the list of species reported for each week. If the list included a report of a bird that was judged to be highly improbable because it occurred at an unprecedented location or time of the year, we deleted that record. Over the years we have had to delete only a few questionable records, and many of these seemed to have been simply the result of a participant accidentally filling in the wrong "bubble" on the form. For example, we looked upon with suspicion—and deleted—records of Common Ravens in a southern Wisconsin county during the summer, especially when the observers had failed to report an American Crow—a species that should have been seen. The raven and crow appear next to each other on the checklist, so we suspected a simple slip of the pen. Similar errors were detected for Boreal Chickadees and Black-capped Chickadees and other species that appeared next to one another on the form.

To double-check the accuracy of the edited data, we also prepared yearly summaries of each participant's reports and returned these summaries to the participant for review. This review process allowed the original observer to help us further in detecting erroneous reports of species.

Participants in the checklist project were unevenly distributed among the 72 counties in Wisconsin, and some individual counties had few participants in them. We attempted to compensate for these deficiencies by combining records from adjacent counties in order to accumulate enough observers and weekly checklists to have a representative sampling effort for the region. Each of the 56 resulting regions had at least 10 participants who collectively contributed at least 250 checklists.

Our analyses of the edited data followed several paths. In order to detect seasonal changes in the abundance of birds in the state, we calculated weekly reporting frequencies for each species. These reporting frequencies were simply the percentage of participants during the week who had reported the species. Preliminary results of this type of analysis were reported by Temple and Temple (1984). These weekly reporting frequencies reveal seasonal variations in the abundance of species.

A second type of analysis was oriented geographically rather than seasonally. We produced range maps for each bird species by calculating its reporting frequencies within each of the 56 regions of the state. These regional reporting frequencies could be calculated for the entire year or, if more appropriate, for just a portion of the year, such as the breeding season. Not only did these range maps show the regions of the state in which the species was found, but in addition the value of the regional reporting frequency provided an index of the regional abundance of the species. Temple and Temple (1986) presented some preliminary results of this type of analysis of the checklist data and concluded that these range maps portrayed quite accurately the geographical patterns of relative abundance within the range of each species.

Seasonal and geographical patterns of abundance can be examined year by year for each year of the checklist project, or all the data can be combined together. In the species accounts this information is based on the combined data from the entire 15 years of the project.

The data from the checklist project can also be used to

LAST NAME (PRINT)

YEAR 19

COUNTY

DID YOU ACTIVELY SEARCH FOR BIRDS THIS WEEK?

YES NO

OBSERVATION FOR WEEK BEGINNING SUNDAY

MONTH

JAN FEB MAR APR MAY JUN JUL AUG SEP OCT NOV DEC

DAY

LOONS	DUCKS (con't)	GROUSE	SANDPIPERS (con't)	OWLS (con't)
○ Red-throated	○ Canvasback	○ Ruffed	○ Semipalmated	○ Great Gray
○ Common	○ Redhead	○ Gr. Prairie Chicken	○ Least	○ Long-eared
	○ Ring-necked	○ Sharp-tailed	○ White-rumped	○ Short-eared
GREBES	○ Greater Scaup		○ Baird's	○ N. Saw-whet
○ Pied-billed	○ Lesser Scaup	**TURKEY**	○ Pectoral	
○ Horned	○ Oldsquaw	○ Wild	○ Dunlin	**NIGHTHAWKS**
○ Red-necked	○ Black Scoter		○ Stilt	○ Common
	○ Surf Scoter	**BOBWHITE**	○ S.-bill. Dowitcher	○ Whip-poor-will
CORMORANTS	○ White-winged Scoter	○ Northern	○ L.-bill. Dowitcher	
○ Double-crested	○ Com. Goldeneye		○ Com. Snipe	**SWIFT**
	○ Bufflehead	**RAILS**	○ Am. Woodcock	○ Chimney
BITTERNS	○ Hooded Merganser	○ Virginia	○ Wilson's Phalarope	
○ American	○ Common Merganser	○ Sora	○ Red-n. Phalarope	**HUMMINGBIRD**
○ Least	○ Red-br. Merganser			○ Ruby-throated
	○ Ruddy	**MOORHEN**	**GULLS**	
HERONS		○ Common	○ Franklin's	**KINGFISHER**
○ Great Blue	**VULTURE**		○ Bonaparte's	○ Belted
○ Great Egret	○ Turkey	**COOT**	○ Ring-billed	
○ Cattle Egret		○ American	○ Herring	**WOODPECKERS**
○ Green-backed	**HAWKS**		○ Glaucous	○ Red-headed
○ Black-cr. Night-	○ Osprey	**CRANE**		○ Red-bellied
○ Yellow-cr. Night-	○ Bald Eagle	○ Sandhill	**TERNS**	○ Yel-h. Sapsucker
	○ Northern Harrier		○ Caspian	○ Downy
SWANS	○ Sharp-Shinned	**PLOVERS**	○ Common	○ Hairy
○ Tundra	○ Cooper's	○ Black-bellied	○ Forster's	○ N. Flicker
○ Mute	○ N. Goshawk	○ Lesser Golden-	○ Black	○ Pileated
	○ Red-shouldered	○ Semipalmated		
GEESE	○ Broad-winged	○ Killdeer	**DOVES**	**FLYCATCHERS**
○ Snow	○ Red-tailed		○ Rock	○ Olive-sided
○ Canada	○ Rough-legged	**SANDPIPERS**	○ Mourning	○ E. Wood-Pewee
	○ American Kestrel	○ Gr. Yellowlegs		○ Yellow-bellied
DUCKS	○ Merlin	○ Lesser Yellowlegs	**CUCKOOS**	○ Acadian
○ Wood	○ Peregrine Falcon	○ Solitary	○ Black-billed	○ Alder
○ Green-winged Teal		○ Willet	○ Yellow-billed	○ Willow
○ Am. Black	**PARTRIDGE**	○ Spotted		○ Least
○ Mallard	○ Gray	○ Upland	**OWLS**	○ Eastern Phoebe
○ Northern Pintail		○ Hudsonian Godwit	○ Com. Barn	○ Great Crested
○ Blue-winged Teal	**PHEASANT**	○ Marbled Godwit	○ E. Screech	○ E. Kingbird
○ Northern Shoveler	○ Ring-necked	○ Ruddy Turnstone	○ Great Horned	
○ Gadwall		○ Red Knot	○ Snowy	**LARK**
○ American Wigeon		○ Sanderling	○ Barred	○ Horned

INSTRUCTIONS

1. Fill in each form completely following the guidelines provided on the general instruction sheet that accompanies these forms.
2. Follow these specific instructions:
   a. Fill in your name.
   b. Fill in the year in which your observations occurred.
   c. Fill in the county code for the county in which you observed the birds; if you observed birds in more than one county, fill in a separate form for each county. County codes are given on the general instruction sheet.
   d. Fill in the month and the date of the Sunday that began the week for which you are reporting. Fill out a separate form for each week.
   e. Answer the question on your birding activities. Answer yes if you specifically went out birding during the week. Answer no if you only observed birds incidentally.
   f. Fill in the birds that you saw or heard during the week. Do not fill in birds that you know are in your area but that you did not actually find.

SWALLOWS	GNATCATCHER	WARBLERS	CARDINALS	BLACKBIRDS
○ Purple Martin	○ Blue-gray	○ Blue-winged	○ Northern Cardinal	○ Bobolink
○ Tree		○ Golden-winged	○ Rose-br. Grosbeak	○ Red-winged
○ N. Rough-winged	**THRUSHES**	○ Tennessee	○ Indigo Bunting	○ E. Meadowlark
○ Bank	○ E. Bluebird	○ Orange-crowned	○ Dickcissel	○ W. Meadowlark
○ Cliff	○ Veery	○ Nashville		○ Yellow-headed
○ Barn	○ Gray-cheeked	○ Northern Parula	**TOWHEE**	○ Rusty
	○ Swainson's	○ Yellow	○ Rufous-sided	○ Brewer's
JAYS	○ Hermit	○ Chestnut-sided		○ Common Grackle
○ Gray	○ Wood	○ Magnolia	**SPARROWS**	○ Brown-headed Cowbird
○ Blue	○ Am. Robin	○ Cape May	○ American Tree	○ Orchard Oriole
		○ Black-thr. Blue	○ Chipping	○ Northern Oriole
CROW	**CATBIRD**	○ Yellow-rumped	○ Clay-colored	
○ American	○ Gray	○ Black-thr. Green	○ Field	**FINCHES**
		○ Blackburnian	○ Vesper	○ Pine Grosbeak
RAVEN	**MOCKINGBIRD**	○ Pine	○ Lark	○ Purple
○ Common	○ Northern	○ Palm	○ Savannah	○ Red Crossbill
		○ Bay-breasted	○ Grasshopper	○ White-w. Crossbill
CHICKADEES	**THRASHER**	○ Blackpoll	○ Henslow's	○ Common Redpoll
○ Black-capped	○ Brown	○ Cerulean	○ Le Conte's	○ Pine Siskin
○ Boreal		○ Black & White	○ Fox	○ Am. Goldfinch
	PIPIT	○ Am. Redstart	○ Song	○ Evening Grosbeak
TITMOUSE	○ Water	○ Prothonotary	○ Lincoln's	○ House
○ Tufted		○ Ovenbird	○ Swamp	
	WAXWINGS	○ N. Waterthrush	○ White-throated	**SPARROW**
NUTHATCHES	○ Bohemian	○ La. Waterthrush	○ White-crowned	○ House
○ Red-breasted	○ Cedar	○ Kentucky	○ Harris'	
○ White-breasted		○ Connecticut	○ Dark-eyed Junco	
	SHRIKES	○ Mourning		
CREEPER	○ Northern	○ Com. Yellowthroat	**LONGSPUR**	
○ Brown	○ Loggerhead	○ Hooded	○ Lapland	
		○ Wilson's		
WRENS	**STARLING**	○ Canada	**BUNTING**	
○ House	○ European	○ Yellow-br. Chat	○ Snow	
○ Winter				
○ Sedge	**VIREOS**	**TANAGER**		
○ Marsh	○ Bell's	○ Scarlet		
	○ Solitary			
KINGLETS	○ Yellow-throated			
○ Golden-crowned	○ Warbling			
○ Ruby-crowned	○ Philadelphia			
	○ Red-eyed			

detect year-to-year changes in the abundance of birds. Reporting frequencies for an entire year or a shorter time period can be compared between different years. Such comparisons have shown that the checklist approach can be a sensitive way of detecting changes in bird populations of Wisconsin (Temple and Temple 1987; Temple and Cary 1990b; Rolley 1992, 1994). We have used regression analyses to describe the overall trends revealed by these data over many years. Comparisons of the long-term trends revealed in the checklist data and trends revealed by other monitoring schemes, such as the North American Breeding Bird Survey and the Christmas Bird Counts, show many close correlations, suggesting that most of the trends are real (Temple and Cary 1990b; Rolley 1994).

Our experience with the Wisconsin Checklist Project convinces us that this new approach to monitoring bird populations has merit. We have shown that the technique is readily accepted by volunteer cooperators and that it produces interpretable data reflecting seasonal, year-to-year, and geographical variations in bird populations. Temple and Cary (1990a) provide a more detailed discussion of the underlying theory and the validity of the technique, but in many ways the results of the project, as presented in this book, must speak for themselves. It is ultimately the bird-watchers of Wisconsin who will decide whether or not the project has produced useful information.

REFERENCES

Bystrak, D. 1981. The North American Breeding Bird Survey. Pp. 34–41. *In* C. J. Ralph and J. M. Scott (eds.). *Estimating the numbers of terrestrial birds.* Studies in Avian Biology No. 6.

Hall, G. A. 1964. Breeding-Bird Censuses—why and how. *Audubon Field Notes* 18:413–416.

Hickey, J. J. 1943. *A guide to bird watching.* Oxford University Press, London.

McCrimmon, D. A. 1977. The collection, management and exchange of information on colonially nesting birds. Pp. 187–196. *In* A. Sprunt, J. Ogden, and S. Winckler (eds.). *Wading Birds.* National Audubon Society, Research Report, No. 7.

Peakall, D. B. 1970. The Eastern Bluebird: its breeding season, clutch size, and nesting success. *Living Bird* 9:239–256.

Robbins, C. S. 1977. Bird atlasing in the United States. *Polish Ecological Studies* 3:325–328.

Robbins, C. S. 1981. Reappraisal of the winter bird-population study technique. Pp. 52–57. *In* C. J. Ralph and J. M. Scott (eds.). *Estimating numbers of terrestrial birds.* Studies in Avian Biology No. 6.

Rolley, R. E. 1992. Wisconsin Checklist Project: 1992 update. *Passenger Pigeon* 54:259–266.

Rolley, R. E. 1994. Wisconsin Checklist Project: 1993 update. *Passenger Pigeon* 56:29–38.

Temple, S. A. 1981. Summarizing remarks: estimating relative abundance. p. 112. *In* C. J. Ralph and J. M. Scott (eds.). *Estimating numbers of terrestrial birds.* Studies in Avian Biology No. 6.

Temple, S. A. 1982. A Wisconsin bird survey based on field checklist information: a WSO research project. *Passenger Pigeon* 44:56–60.

Temple, S. A. 1996. The checklist connection. *Living Bird Quarterly* 15:7–13.

Temple, S. A., and J. R. Cary. 1987. Climatic effects on year-to-year variations in migration phenology: a WSO research project. *Passenger Pigeon* 49:70–75.

Temple, S. A., and J. R. Cary. 1990a. Description of the Wisconsin Checklist Project. *US Fish and Wildlife Service Biological Report* 90:14–17.

Temple, S. A., and J. R. Cary. 1990b. Using checklist records to reveal trends in bird populations. *US Fish and Wildlife Service Biological Report* 90:98–104.

Temple, S. A., and B. L. Temple. 1976. Avian population trends in central New York state, 1935–72. *Bird Banding* 47:238–257.

Temple, S. A., and A. J. Temple. 1984. Results of using checklist-records to monitor Wisconsin birds: a WSO research project. *Passenger Pigeon* 46:61–70.

Temple, S. A., and A. J. Temple. 1986. Geographic distributions and patterns of relative abundance of Wisconsin birds: a WSO research project. *Passenger Pigeon* 48:58–68.

Temple, S. A., and A. J. Temple. 1987. Detecting year-to-year changes in bird populations with checklist records: a WSO research project. *Passenger Pigeon* 49:158–162.

Index